The Plimpton Papers —
Law and Diplomacy

Francis Plimpton in a seminar on "Justice and Society" at the Aspen Institute of Humanistic Studies in 1980.

The Plimpton Papers — Law and Diplomacy

The Credibility of Institutions, Policies and Leadership
Volume 8

Collected and Edited by
Pauline Ames Plimpton

Foreword by
George Plimpton

University Press of America
Lanham ● New York ● London

Library of Congress Cataloging-in-Publication Data

Plimpton, Francis T.P. (Francis Taylor Pearsons),
    1900-1983.
    The Plimpton papers—law and diplomacy.

    (The Credibility of institutions, policies and
leadership; v. 8)
    "Co-published by arrangement with the White Burkett
Miller Center of Public Affairs, University of
Virginia"—T.p. verso.
    Includes index.
    1. Law—United States—Addresses, essays, lectures.
2. Diplomacy—Addresses, essays, lectures.
I. Plimpton, Pauline Ames, 1901-   . II. Title.
II. Series.
KF213.P55P56   1985   349.73'092'4   85-11275
                        347.300924
    ISBN 0-8191-4783-4 (alk. paper)
    ISBN 0-8191-4784-2 (pbk. : alk. paper)

THE CREDIBILITY OF INSTITUTIONS, POLICIES AND LEADERSHIP
A Series funded by the Hewlett Foundation
Kenneth W. Thompson, *Series Editor*

Also by Pauline Ames Plimpton

Orchids at Christmas

The Ancestry of Blanche Butler Ames
  and Adelbert Ames

Oakes Ames – Jottings of a Harvard Botanist

Apostrophe

Oh father Zeus who guides the ever-mounting sun,
    Why could you not have granted men two lives, the one
To pass in love and laughter, the other in toil and strain?
    For then perhaps we'd do the drudging first, and live
    A life at a time, content to know the future would give
Fulfillment to our dreams. But do we labor in vain?

For Fate decrees we live but once, too brief a time
For us to more than glimpse the heights, and start the climb,
Unknowing when the path may stop—or lead to the plain.
    Two lives are one, so intermingled and entwined
    We cannot choose or pick, but only hope to find
Reward in toil itself, and pleasure in our pain.

Francis Plimpton
Amherst Writing
1922

Acknowledgments

I am grateful to Evan Thomas, the distinguished editor of Harper & Row and then of W. W. Norton, whose idea it was that this book should be written; to Prof. Kenneth Thompson of the University of Virginia for his interest and editorial advice; and especially to our son, George Plimpton, who has helped me all along the way arranging and editing and always urging me to work harder.

I thank, also, all the friends whose faces have lit up at hearing of a book about Francis and thus have given me inspiration.

I am indebted to Patricia Ryan and Jan Granger Wikstrom in the preparation of the manuscript and in dealing with all the mechanical problems of a mass of material.

Table of Contents

Foreword

It was always a pleasure to hear my father speak. Whatever the occasion it invariably seemed to me that a fine anticipatory hum was in the air when the chairs were pushed back, the last of the demi-tasse cups were removed, and whoever was to introduce father tapped his water glass for quiet. Part of it was that his audience—at least those of it who were aware of his reputation—knew that they were in for a display of the perfect balance of erudition, wit, and good sense that is provided by a classic speech. Even *before* his remarks, father displayed an ease and confidence; seated at the dais, he was able to carry on an animated conversation with his dinner partners, whereas most dinner speakers I've noticed stare into the middle distance, tend to pick at their food and wish they were somewhere else.

Father never practiced his speeches on anyone. Once, mother had suggested that he try them out on her. Apparently, her father, Oakes Ames, who as head of the botany department at Harvard University was famous for his lectures, liked to rehearse in front of *his* wife. Father tried it. Subsequently he said that it had been his most embarrassing moment as an orator, and he never involved mother again. The speeches were as fresh to her when they were delivered as they were to the rest of the audience—a typical example being the little speech, "In Praise Of Polygamy" which was inspired by a magazine article she read to him on a drive up to Amherst and was formulated soundlessly in his mind as he sat beside her in the car.

This is not to suggest that he did not have his sources. Close at hand when he sat down to compose a speech was a special reference library, many of the volumes duplicated so that whether he was sitting at his desk at Debevoise & Plimpton, or in the New York apartment, or in the country at West Hills, he could reach for inspiration. The

collection might serve as a model for a public speaker's shelf: among
the various dictionaries, thesauri and encyclopedias were *Laugh Day*
by Bennett Cerf, *A Practical Dictionary of Rhymes* by Lawrence Hol-
ofcener, Benjamin N. Cardozo's *Memorial Lectures, 100th Anniversary
Edition*, the *Reader's Digest Treasury of Wit and Humor, Podium Humor* by James C. Humes, Leon Harris' *The Fine Art of Political Wit*
(with a colophon of a feathered dart on the spine), Strunk and White's
The Elements of Style, Brewer's *Dictionary of Phrase and Fable*, the
Public Speaker's Treasure Chest, An Almanac of Words at Play by
Willard R. Espy, and, of all things, Mao Tse-tung's *Little Red Book*.

Then, father carried a time-worn black foldback notebook which he
would produce from an inside coatpocket from time to time for reference, or to make a note in his small, meticulous handwriting. I had
always assumed he kept a treasure-trove in its pages of sayings, quips,
notions, perhaps a joke or two which would eventually turn up in a
speech. Not at all. I found only one quotation . . . in Greek, which he
translates:

For when is good-will greater
Than from a guest to host?

But the rest of the notebook does offer a key to the ordered patterns
of my father's life—a kind of Baedeker of his activities and interests.
Lists predominate—where to buy clothes in Ireland (*tweeds*—Kevin
and Howdin); dine in Italy (*Milan:* Aldo, via della Maddelini—fish);
what wines to buy and their gradations (Red Burgundies . . . *Great!:*
Chambertin, Clos de Bèze, Clos de Tart, Musigny, etc. *Fine:* Gevrez
Chambertin, Morey-Saint Denis, etc.). A separate page is devoted to
California wines.

Two pages are entitled GOLF, the other TENNIS—a kind of check-
list to review before father went out to play. Among his golfing self-
admonitions: "Stay on heels—hit down on irons—bring club straight
back from address. *Putting*—do with wrists, not arms—follow through—
head still! ! !" etc.

The tennis self-instructions are shorter and limited to the serve: ". . .
throw ball forward—hit on top of it—*get it over the net*", etc. . . . this
last not a dictum that father kept to himself. How often I have heard
those words from him after the misery of my serving a double-fault!

The rest of the book is devoted to lists of acquaintances categorized
by locations: People – London; People – Italy; People – Jamaica; People
– U.N.; People – Greece; People – Detroit; People – Far East, and so
forth. The lists are extensive (twenty friends in Jamaica, for example,

a place I doubt he visited more than three or four times) and a browse through them, flipping the pages thick with names, is to find the upper echelons of political, business, social, and artistic representatives from each locale.

While the notebook was obviously not a source for his talks, he did keep in the top drawer of his office desk a file entitled Speech Material. I have it in front of me—largely tear-sheets of other people's speeches: Lord Caradon's speech before the Pilgrims (1965); Professor Paul A. Freund's speech before the American Law Institute (1975); Freund again, this time with a speech entitled "The Moral Education of the Lawyer;" a list of Felix Frankfurter's more memorable quotes; a commencement address by James B. Reston (at Smith College in the spring of 1961); a few scraps of paper with notes on them in father's hand (a stanza from Walt Whitman's "Leaves of Grass", a phrase of Nietzsche's); a wall calendar in which the months are accompanied by quotations from Lord Russell (on Thought) to H.G. Wells (on Insubordination); an article on famous quips (*Lord Sandwich:* "Really, Mr. Wilkes, I don't know whether you'll die on the gallows or of the pox." *John Wilkes:* "That depends, my lord, upon whether I embrace your principles or your mistress.").

Irresistible among the contents in the Speech Material file is the following book review (marked *authentic*) which originally appeared in *Field and Stream:*

Although written many years ago, Lady Chatterley's Lover has just been reissued by Grove Press, and this fictional account of the day to day life of an English gamekeeper is still of considerable interest to outdoor-minded readers . . . as it contains many passages on pheasant raising, the apprehension of poachers, ways to control vermin, and other chores and duties of the professional gamekeeper.

Unfortunately, one is obliged to wade through many pages of extraneous material in order to discover and savor these sidelights on the management of a Midlands shooting estate, and in this reviewer's opinion, this book cannot take the place of J.R. Miller's *Practical Gamekeeping.*

I do not recall this particular item, however delightful, turning up in one of father's speeches. Indeed, except for the occasional underlined passage (especially in the Freund talks), it does not appear that he used very much from the Speech Material folder.

In fact, a secretary who was with him for many years recalls that while father dictated his speeches to her, he rarely referred to any notes, or even to the reference books he had available. "It all seemed to be stored in his mind," she told me. "He would walk by my desk and tell me that he had another speech to give to so-and-so. I'd give a small, inward groan because I knew it was going to be a long day. But it was never a boring day. I never ceased to marvel at his mental feats of memory and organization."

The typed speeches which father took to the podium have an odd cipher system on the pages which gives no clues as to how it worked. Almost every word is underlined with a heavy pencil-stroke—too many to suggest that certain words were to be emphasized as he spoke them. My guess is that before every speech, father read it over with great care, underlining words as a proofreader does, and in the process was able to commit most of the speech to memory. Certainly, one remembers about father's speeches that for considerable stretches he would look out at his audience as he talked with only an occasional glance down at his text. Many public speakers have such systems: Mark Twain's was to arrange the tableware, forks, knives, salt-cellars and so forth, in some prearranged pattern at his dinner place, which would serve to remind him of the various topics, and in the proper order, which he wished to discuss. I have often wondered what the sudden removal by an overfastidious waiter of these mnemonic devices would have done to the smooth flow of his words.

Father once said in an interview that he became a lawyer because he could not think of what else to do. Very likely, he could have been a writer, an editor, a teacher, or even a poet. Certainly his great gift was that of communication with others. The speeches in this volume are mostly restricted to among those he devoted to the subjects of law and diplomacy—as one can tell from the title. Would room were available for some of the others! An upstairs closet in my mother's New York apartment is overcrowded by cardboard boxes filled with folders containing a wide variety of talks. Many of them turn out to be addresses he gave at educational institutions—schools, colleges, graduate schools. What is striking about them is that there is never any condescension whatever to the makeup or age of his audience. An appropriate quotation from Horace is as likely to turn up in a talk to a gathering of schoolboys as in a speech to the members of a Bar Association. Inevitably, his audience is asked to enjoy his level of intellect and wit.

And yet, of all the exchanges with an audience, the one I remember with a particular poignancy was between my father and mother . . . a communication which actually did not contain a single word! The incident took place during ceremonies in the U.N.'s General Assembly hall at which father officially took his position as a U.S. Ambassador to that body. Father had reached an exalted position in an organization in which—theoretically at least—the importance of communication is supreme. The ceremony was impressive and rather grand. At its conclusion, I noticed father give a small, very discreet thumbs-up gesture, not noticeable to anyone who had not been forewarned. Mother and I were sitting together in the gallery. Mother had tipped me off. I saw father's thumb come up, alongside the gold chain across his vest. I caught mother smiling, and then she did the same—even more shyly. They were justifiably very proud of each other.

Mother is responsible for producing this volume. Because of the nature of the book's subject, there is not enough of her in it. Originally, when there was freer rein, she wanted to call the book *Our Lives Were Blessed,* lines quoted in one of Anne Lindbergh's books—which is a truer reflection of the full and rewarding experience she and father had together from the day they met in 1922.

—George Plimpton

Introduction

Francis Taylor Pearsons Plimpton (he used the two middle initials, Francis T. P. Plimpton) was a true New Yorker. He was born on December 7, 1900, on Thirty-Third Street in New York. His mother, Frances Taylor Pearsons, had died when he was born and he was given her name. The adjective most used to describe her was "beautiful". She graduated from Wellesley in 1884, was president of her class and President of the Wellesley Club of New York. She came from Holyoke, Massachusetts, where her father, Judge W. B. C. Pearsons had been Mayor; her mother was a direct descendant of Edward Taylor, known as "the first American poet" of Westfield, Massachusetts.

Francis' father, George Arthur Plimpton, was one of nine children, six brothers and three sisters, all of whom grew up in Walpole, Massachusetts. An ancestor was a Sergeant John Plimpton, who was burned at the stake by the Indians after the Deerfield Massacre in 1677.

George Arthur Plimpton was a publisher of educational textbooks. Although his father died when he was young, his mother had been able to send him to Exeter, then Amherst, and through a year of Harvard Law School. She then gave him a thousand dollars to fend for himself. He became a book salesman for Ginn & Co. (a publishing house devoted entirely to textbooks), selling schoolbooks throughout the South. He ended up becoming a member of the firm in 1882 and at Edwin Ginn's death, the Senior Partner and then Head of the Firm in New York.

At his wife's death in 1900, he was left to bring up his little boy alone. In the earliest years, the maternal grandmother, Sarah Taylor Pearsons, presided over the household and, as time went on, nurses or governesses were provided to care for him. Francis grew up in Murray Hill in Manhattan in the winters and he spent the summers at the Lewis Farm in Walpole, Massachusetts, a rather lonely child, mainly in the company of grown-ups. He has told me of the interesting "strays" his father (a widower for seventeen years) would bring home for Sunday breakfast or lunch. He particularly remembered one of his father's closest friends, Professor David Eugene Smith of Teachers College, Columbia, a little, short, stocky man, very learned, who was the author of "Rara Arithmetica."

Combining his avocation with his vocation, George Arthur collected educational manuscripts and early textbooks such as hornbooks (an early kind of primer made of transparent horn) and pre-1600 arithmetics. He kept the most valuable books in a vault under his house at 61 Park Avenue in New York and would bring them up to his library to display to interested groups whom he inevitably offered ice cream and after dinner coffee. When he lectured at universities, he carried examples from his collection in a cardboard suitcase.

A story is told about Mr. Plimpton, the collector. He was a friend of Henry Clay Folger, responsible for the Folger Shakespeare Library in Washington. The two gentlemen met on the street one day. Mr. Plimpton remarked that he noticed that Queen Elizabeth I's corsets were for sale and that he had written over for them. Mr. Folger replied, "I've got them, I cabled!"

I shall never forget seeing George Arthur Plimpton in action for the first time. Bringing all kinds of treasures through customs, he was showing the customs agent a Papal Bull with such delight and concentration that the agent was completely distracted from the business at hand. Probably, in his astonishment at a bull being anything but bovine, he allowed everything through.

Overall, the collector amassed 1600 manuscripts (he called them "the tools of learning") and donated them to Columbia University before his death. From his study of these manuscripts he wrote two books, "The Education of Shakespeare", which was such a success that he followed it with "The Education of Chaucer."

George Arthur Plimpton did not restrict his collecting to early educational artifacts. He collected all sorts and conditions of things. In memory of Francis' mother, who was devoted to Italian literature, he presented Wellesley College, her alma mater, with a library of original and early Italian authors. His French and Indian Wars Collection, relating particularly to Lord Jeffrey Amherst, he gave to Amherst College; to Phillips Exeter Academy he donated his considerable collection of documents from the pre-Civil War South. Among interesting items were the log book of the master of an African slave trader and the will of a southern gentleman who recited that due to the war he had no property to leave, but that he gave, devised and bequeathed to all of his descendants, forever, an undying hatred of the Yankee nation.

Another unique collection was of cigar store wooden Indians. These have now become virtually unobtainable, but, with an unerring eye for collectibles, he would approach guileless cigar store proprietors and offer to take the wooden Indians from their steps without charge. The result was an imposing collection around the courtyard of the Lewis Farm. Once he incautiously put one of the gaily colored tribe in the wood peering out at a nearby equestrain statue of an armed Puritan. Although promptly abducted by some of the local youths, it was safely recovered after the insertion of a notice in the local paper: "lost, strayed or stolen—one wooden Indian."

Quite late in life he began a collection of contemporary portraits of English authors, which increased into almost fifty items, ranging from the outstanding Occleve portrait of Chaucer, purchased at the Baroness Burdett Coutts sale in London, through a somewhat dubious 1610 portrait of Shakespeare at the age of 46 by one Lynde (otherwise unknown).

Francis went to Phillips Exeter Academy at thirteen, his father's school. His interest in writing began on the Exeter Monthly and while working for the Exonian, the School paper, only beaten for the top position on the latter by John Cowles, one of his best friends, whose father owned the *Des Moines Register* and *Tribune*. John Cowles, himself, eventually became the publisher of the *Minneapolis Star Tribune*.

In one of his speeches, Francis describes his teachers at Exeter.

> The most formidable of the good teachers were those in Latin, and formidable they were. Perhaps the language, formidable itself in its disciplined exactness, was responsible, or possibly the magisterial majesty of Roman law, but the triumvirate of Clark, Kirtland and Gillespie were as terrifying a set of triumvirs as any member of the plebs (or the prep class) ever bowed down before.
>
> Doctor Clark was a solid, heavy, gray man, with a grayish moustache and grayish beard, invariably dressed in dark clothes with a white starched wing collar appearing on the two sides of his beard. A heavy gold watch chain and fob stretched in two loops across an ample waistcoat. A dignified gray fedora, creased down the middle, sat stiff

and upright on his head as he walked with measured portly steps from Dunbar to the Academy Building.

In the classroom he sat forbiddingly immobile behind a wooden desk on the raised platform, backed by a blackboard and gloomy prints of the Forum, facing the 30 or so boys who in those unenlightened days made up a class. The resonant twang with which he called on his victims to recite was by itself enough to quail any mind, however well prepared for the day's travail of 50 lines (was it 50?) of the Aeneid, and no sound has ever been as devastating as the harsh bark, "Sit down, you don't know what you're talking about" which collapsed the unprepared into slumped disgrace.

I suspect that Pop Clark, as for no discoverable reason he was known, was in private a kind husband and a tolerant parent, but in Latin 2 and Latin 3 there was no evidence of any such non-Roman frailties. Yet, to this day I can remember the time when for once (it was probably only once) I had turned myself inside out to produce a perfect translation of those 50 lines and he let me recite on and on without his usual abrupt corrections, and then said, quietly, "You have done enough, Plimpton—next . . . " Not a word of praise, but the quiet tone and not being interrupted were rewards I still treasure from among memories of his sarcastic harassment of the unprepared, myself at other times included.

Professor Kirtland, known as Squint by reason of what must have been the most extreme case of internal strabismus in medical history, was also bearded, with close cropped, slightly curled black whiskers under his rimless oval spectacles that framed black eyes so at cross purposes that rows of boys would all feel they were being simultaneously and searchingly peered at.

The author of Kirtland's Latin Grammar, the Holy Writ of that irritatingly grammatical tongue, was Olympian in his uncompromising insistence on exactness and firm impatience with error. Cicero's orations seemed intricate mechanisms of interrelated cams and shafts that could only be correctly taken apart (translated) by a watchmaker bent over the microscope screwed into his right eye.

Doctor Gillespie, a large, bald-domed man with auburn

moustache and beard—inevitably known as Pink Whiskers—was by comparison (but only by comparison) somewhat less forbidding; the austere precision with which he corrected ineptitude had in it a hint of tolerance of juvenile human imperfection.

Exeter Greek was something else. The department, in the person of Dr. Arthur Gardner Leacock, was as different from the Messrs. Clark, Kirtland, et al as Sappho's lyrics are from Caesar's Gallic Wars. The good Doctor was an impeccably groomed, trimly Van Dyck moustached and bearded gentleman of courtly and benevolent charm, who beneath hair meticulously parted in the middle, looked at you pleasantly through rimless spectacles over a high and spotlessly white starched collar. Walking down Front Street with a debonair stick in one hand and Mrs. Leacock on his arm, toward his perfectly proportioned white house, he was the very glass of quiet fashion—even though the petitely vivacious Mrs. Leacock's somewhat general (for 1917) applications of rouge and her gay-colored frocks convinced all Exonians that she was an ex-Ziegfield Follies girl.

Dr. Leacock was a pleasure in class. If a Lower Middler's translation of the Gospel according to St. Mark bore a striking resemblance to the King James version, the good Doctor was benignly tolerant. He was patient with those who stumbled over gerundives, and dealt with the unprepared more in sorrow than in anger. Xenophon's Anabasis he related to the then current campaigns in Asia Minor, and the Illiad he related to Schliemann's Troy and not to grammatical abnormalities. The language itself he subordinated to what the language was about.

Those of us who sat at Dr. Leacock's feet have most probably forgotten all our Greek, but we will never forget the enriching influence of a very cultivated gentleman.

Years later, at a much applauded speech at an Exeter dinner in New York, Francis attacked the old form of education and said that he thought eight years of Latin and Greek had been a waste of time. After his speech, Lewis Perry, (the principal of Exeter) got up and said, "If Francis Plimpton had not had eight years of Latin and Greek, I doubt if he could have made such a good speech."

Francis was elected a Trustee of Exeter in the spring of 1935; he remained a Trustee until 1965, being President of the Board for the last ten years of his tenure. His life was a natural continuum of his father's in a striking way. Now, in the Assembly Building, the portraits of George Arthur Plimpton, class of 1873, and of his son, class of 1917, hang on the left side of the stage opposite the plaque for those lost in the two world wars.

In the Fall of 1917 Francis entered Amherst. He was President of his class for two years and well-known to the girls who went over to the Fraternity tea dances, which, I might add, I did not do. Although Francis does not remember me at Smith, I recall the first time I ever saw him. He was sitting in a box at the Academy of Music in Northampton. There was a repertory company in town at the time, putting on a different play every week from Ibsen to Barrie. Francis was wearing a pale blue woolen suit with a Norfolk jacket. He has since admitted that that suit was a mistake.

At Amherst, Francis continued his literary bent. He worked on the Amherst Student and was editor-in-chief of Amherst Writing, the college literary publication. He was also president of Phi Beta Kappa, and of a less reputable, illegal drinking society known as Kappa Beta Phi. He carried the charms representing both of these societies on his gold watch chain. He wore them throughout his life, his watch in one pocket of his vest and in the other a gold knife and pencil given him by his father on his twenty-first birthday. On some occasions he concealed the honorary keys, I never quite knew why.

Here are Francis' words, thinking back to Amherst and Alexander Meiklejohn, who was President at that time:

> How can any of us forget that small, trim, spare frame, the domed forehead, the glint of the spectacles and of the eyes behind them, the prim Scottish precision of his words, the understated oblique meaningfulness of what he said, pregnant with unspoken implication. One felt an inner lift from the uncompromising, undeviating directness of his insistence on the search for the truth no matter where that search might lead.
>
> And the men he brought to the College—Gettell, who taught that eye-opening introduction to learning known as Social and Economic Institutions and combined it with

coaching that unforgettable football team that in our junior year—the Centennial year—beat Williams' All-American Benny Boyton 14–7; Walter Stewart, whose clarity of mind made him adviser to the Bank of England; Walter Hamilton, whose provocative probing of labor and labor law made him a top Yale Law School Professor and afterward a Washington luminary; Stark Young, who with his sophisticated Southern urbanity, became a leading drama critic and literary light— and many others.

There was, at least for some of us some of the time, an incandescent electric quality about the Meiklejohn era, a stimulating excitement about the pursuit of knowledge.

Francis' interest in Amherst continued throughout his life. In the thirties, he was made chairman of the Alumni Fund and in 1939, after his father's death and the year his brother Calvin (his father had married again in 1917 and Calvin and later a sister, Emily, were born) graduated from Amherst, he became a life Trustee and a most devoted one.

Every fall we would drive up through the Connecticut valley to Trustees' meetings. During one of these drives to Amherst in 1957, Francis composed one of his most famous speeches. He delivered his remarks extemporaneously in the Amherst Chapel. I was as surprised and charmed as everyone else. It was subsequently reprinted in Walter Lippmann's column and in a little pamphlet printed by Frank Altschul's Overbrook Press, and in a few anthologies. It has had by far and away the most reprints at the Overbrook Press. He called it "In Praise of Polygamy."

Yesterday afternoon, driving up from New York, I was subjected to a most distressing experience—my wife read me the leading article in this month's Harper's. It is by a member of the class of 1927 by the name of Charles Woolsey Cole, the President of this college. It is entitled "American Youth Goes Monogamous."

The article portrays, gentlemen, the state of *your* mores, and, if I may say so, a most lamentable state it is. It appears that each of you fastens upon one unfortunate female, and, forsaking all others, brings her and her alone to each game, each cocktail party, each dance. Furthermore, the hapless creature has to dance with you, and you alone, during the long hours of low and mournful peripatetics which you appear to believe constitutes dancing. This drab process is, I understand, known as "going steady"—a clear violation not only of English grammar, but also of the most elementary principles of biology.

It is punctuated, according to your President, by a gruesome ceremony known as "pinning," in which the female bosom is decorated with miscellaneous jewelry to the accompaniment of solemn tribal chants. This of course leads, with the inevitability of Greek tragedy, to matrimony.

Now I hasten to say that I have nothing against matrimony. After all, in every man's life a certain number of things go wrong which in good conscience one really can't blame on the government; also, it is wonderful to have a wife to stand by you in all the troubles you wouldn't have got into if you hadn't married her.

But that isn't the point; the point is, what is to become of the spirit of scientific inquiry? What is to become of the controlled experiment, the controlled experiment which forms the very basis of the advancement of knowledge? Indeed, what is to become of the uncontrolled experiment? Where is natural selection, where is survival of the fittest, where is the evolution of the race if you young males meekly submit to the inexorably monogamous possessiveness of the first female who deigns to notice you?

If I am not mistaken, Thomas Edison tried out some 178 different substances before he finally selected one as the best filament for the electric light bulb. Am I to understand, gentlemen, that his shining example means nothing to you, that you regard good procreation as less important than good illumination?

I am reminded of the episode of Reed Smoot, the first Senator to be elected from Utah. He was a Mormon, and several Senators protested to Boies Penrose, then the leader of the Senate, that he should not be allowed to take his seat. Penrose asked whether Smoot had more than one wife and, on being told that he had only one, looked out over the Senate and said: "Well, I don't see why we can't get along just as well with a polygamist who doesn't polyg as we do with a lot of monogamists who don't monog!"

Now, gentlemen, since I am a lawyer you will not want me to neglect the legal aspects of your situation, and I am bound to say they are serious. Suppose that one of you imports a lady to these precincts, and let us further suppose that she is, in the fine old legal phrase, "clothed with the public interest." What happens? The public interest, whether due to clothes or lack of clothes, is intense, but what do you do? Flouting that public interest you suppress all competition and tend to create a monopoly. Needless to say, gentlemen, this is an unlawful restraint of trade and a flagrant and willful violation of the Sherman Act (and perhaps of the Mann Act), subjecting you to servitude that is penal as well as matrimonial and to triple damage suits at the hands of your aggrieved competitors.

Gentlemen, such a sad state of monotonous monogamy has not always prevailed in this fairest of colleges. In "the golden haze of (my) college days" (deathless phrase), a man who brought the same girl to every dance was rightfully regarded as a man without resources, without imagination, without *élan vital*. It was a matter of pride with us to provide ourselves and our friends and admirers with the spice of variety—and the more variety and, may I say, the more spice, the more the admirers. For one dance, a charmer from Smith; for the next, a lithe damsel from Mt. Holyoke; for the next a lissome lass from Poughkeepsie; and glorious climax, a debutante of glow and glamour from the ormolu ballroom of the now defunct Ritz Carlton. If we did any pinning, it was to pin them in a corner and not for any purpose connected with the decorative arts.

And, gentlemen, we did not shrink from fair competition, the life of trade. The American spirit of free enterprise had free play, and play it did. The lordly stag now, alas, almost extinct, was then monarch of all he surveyed, as he enjoyed what should be the inalienable rights of every young American male, the rights of life, liberty, and the happiness of pursuit.

Yes, those were great days, and I commend to you, gentlemen, the lessons of that glorious past. Let not these honored traditions fade! Undergraduates of the World, arise— you have nothing to lose but your silk and nylon chains!

What pleased Francis most about his chapel speech was that at a reception at the White House for new appointees (when he was appointed an Ambassador to the U.N.), Kenneth Galbraith, who had been nominated Ambassador to India, told him that he would rather have written "In Praise of Polygamy" than any work of his own.

From Amherst, Francis went to the Harvard Law School, entering with the class of 1925. There he made friends who were to mean a great deal to him later on. The class of 1925 was indeed an unusual class. Francis' two roommates in his second year were Adlai Stevenson, perhaps one of the least likely of its members to go on to such an illustrious career (he ended up failing two courses because of the pressure of family matters, took a year out and finally got his law degree at Northwestern), and Charles Denby, a nephew of the Secretary of the Navy. Also in his class were Thomas Corcoran, a well-known Washington lawyer, co-author of the Securities Acts of 1933 and 1934, influential advisor to a succession of Presidents and known as Tommy the Cork; Ammi Cutter, a Justice of the Supreme Judicial Court of Massachusetts; J. Edward Lumbard, Chief Judge of the U.S. Court of Appeals for the Second Circuit and Bethuel Webster, a President of the Association of the Bar of the City of New York.

Throughout his law school years, Francis was still ambivalent about his future career; he continued to try his hand at writing. During his third year Walter Lippmann, who was the editor of the editorial page of the New York *World*, wrote Felix Frankfurter that the world—with a small "w"—was getting so full of legal complications that the *World*—with a capital "W"—should add a legally trained mind to its editorial board, and asked for any suggestions. Frankfurter recommended Francis. During his Christmas vacation, Francis spent a day with Lippmann, who cross-examined him as to his qualifications and introduced him to Herbert Bayard Swope, Alexander Woolcott, Heywood Broun, Franklin P. Adams (F.P.A.) and other New York *World* luminaries. He was asked to write some editorials from Cambridge.

Francis wrote four, of which the *World* printed two—one on a Supreme Court decision on Chicago's tampering with the level of the Great Lakes, and the other on a court decision on kosher food. Lippmann then wrote regretfully that the *World* had decided to retain as its consultant, Thomas Reed Powell, then of Columbia Law School and a distinguished authority on consitutional law. The *World* folded a few years later, so Francis did not have to mourn his lost journalistic career for very long.

Perhaps as a result of meeting Franklin P. Adams, Francis continued to send a number of contributions to the Conning Tower, the F.P.A. column in the *World*, principally translations from the Greek anthologies, refuting Mr. Justice Oliver Wendell Holmes, who was supposed to have said, "No gentlemen needs to know Greek, he only needs to have forgotten it."

But perhaps Francis' best known literary accomplishment, while at Law School, was a satirical poem about the faculty called "In Personam" (worked on, he always said, to the detriment of his marks). He read it at the 1925 Christmas dinner of the Lincoln's Inn Society, to the great amusement of his audience, which included the Law Faculty. So many people wanted copies that the satire was printed up in a little book by the Dunster House Bookshop for two dollars. (For his fiftieth reunion it was reprinted by the Law School as "Reunion Runes.") Many years later, Adlai Stevenson said he wouldn't take a hundred dollars for his copy. The verse Francis would recite if pressed was about Felix Frankfurter:

> "You learn no law in 'Public U'—
> That is its fascination—
> But Felix gives a point of view
> And pleasant conversation."

He recounted that after the Lincoln's Inn dinner, he met Dean Roscoe Pound on the street in Cambridge and was scolded, "I spent ten years trying to persuade the alumni that Felix Frankfurter was a good teacher, and you've ruined it all in one afternoon."

Francis made his choice of law firms during the summer after his graduation in 1925. He decided on Root, Clark, Buckner, Howland and Ballantine, one of the up-and-coming firms. Elihu Root was the son of the Secretary of War and later on in life painted what Francis called "very nude nudes" which were often exhibited at the Century Club. Grenville Clark was a lawyer famous for his liberal leanings. Emory Buckner was U.S. Attorney for the Southern District of New York and a noted trial lawyer. Francis remembers Silas Howland, a skillful advisor, for his idiosyncrasy of going to The Down Town Association for lunch and keeping his hat on throughout. Arthur Ballantine was Under Secretary of the Treasury under Hoover and a prominent tax lawyer.

Once settled in his law firm, Francis was secure enough to take on a bride. We had met on a boat from Liverpool to Boston, the Cunard Line "Tyrrhenia," in 1922, the year we both graduated from college, Smith and Amherst.

The extraordinary thing was that we discovered that we lived only about twelve miles apart—the Plimptons' ancestral farm in Walpole and my father's country house in North Easton, Massachusetts. Actually, the road was so bad, almost a wood-road, between the Farm and my father's back entrance, that I'm sure Francis broke the springs of his car when he came to call and play tennis. We were a tennis family, the court always in use, people playing and watching.

In 1926, mother and father and my sister, Evelyn, and I had journeyed to New York and had sailed on a Caribbean cruise on the "S.S. Columbus." It was an education to travel with them—my father, Oakes Ames, a professor of Botany at Harvard, an authority on orchids and my mother, Blanche Ames Ames, a foremost botanical artist, portrait painter and activist. Her drawings or etchings illustrate her husband's botanical books. The two were interested in the flora and economic products of every island or country that we visited. They complemented each other in such a way that it was my ambition to have a marriage like theirs. Adding to my enjoyment of the trip, Francis had given the purser letters for me, one for every day of the cruise—a most effective manner of devotion. I'm sure he sat up all night to do this! On our return, as we stood on the dock, he presented me with an engagement ring.

We were married on June 4, 1926 under the white wisteria in the rock garden at Borderland, North Easton, Massachusetts, where I grew up. The Unitarian minister from the lovely North Easton church, famous for its LaFarge window, officiated.

We had planned to go on our honeymoon to the Island of Jersey where we expected to spend a few bucolic days on the grassy cliffs with sea gulls flying overhead. Arriving in London in the middle of a general strike, nothing was running including the ferries to Jersey. We managed to get to Bournemouth, a sad seaside town, walking the boardwalk in the rain until we were able to get on a steamer, third class. Separated, the women on one deck and the men on another, the honeymoon was not working out as we expected. The bunks had rough blankets and no sheets and everyone was seasick.

The Island of Jersey was not at all what we imagined either. Saint Helier turned out to be a town with atrocious weather and bad food. To add to our problems, the day after we arrived we received a cable from Francis' law firm, Root, Clark (a forewarning perhaps of what we were to expect from the law) that a client of theirs was approaching the Island of Jersey in a large yacht for legal advice from Francis—Francis only a year out of law school! The client was an English lawyer who had won great sums at the racetrack and was living in Spain trying to avoid British taxes.

When we got out to the countryside to play golf, he would walk along beside us. He had a peculiar habit of speaking and then repeating exactly the same words in a lower tone, almost a whisper. At the end of the day, he invited us on his yacht and gave us champagne and strawberries.

We went on to visit the Italian Lakes, sailed down the Rhine and eventually embarked from Rotterdam to New York. I instinctively knew that no matter how much I might prefer to live in the less complicated world of Boston, Francis was going to pursue his law career in New York.

PART ONE

The Law

The Law

Francis labored hard at Root, Clark, mainly in corporate law. In those days, the law was indeed a jealous mistress. Lawyers customarily worked every Saturday until eventually they went to their offices every other Saturday; now they rarely work on Saturdays. Francis would usually enter our door for dinner at seven-thirty with a briefcase full of work. One summer I spent in Massachusetts with our two little boys. Francis was only able to spend the Fourth of July and Labor Day with us. As a result, we settled on Long Island for our country home, within commuting distance of New York.

In 1929, the firm surprised Francis by assigning him to the Paris office to take the place of Cloyd Laporte, one of the leading younger partners and a predecessor of Francis as Chairman of the New York City Board of Ethics. So, in January of 1930, on two weeks' notice, we sailed for Paris with our two little boys on the "S.S. Berengaria." We settled into a delectable apartment on the Champs de Mars for a two-year stint. Francis suddenly found himself running Root, Clark's office in Paris with one law clerk, which was a tremendous responsibility for a thirty-year-old lawyer. He did have an excellent French accent acquired at a Swiss camp when he was fourteen and an ear for language which stood him in good stead. Here he describes some of the cases he worked on—remembered and recounted in the 1980's.

> I started out with a forty million dollar financing of the Royal Dutch Company debentures for Dillon Read—the first financing that the Company had ever done with any American banking firm. It necessitated long trips to The Hague and London. The Dutch were fairly friendly, but when they discovered that I was not a member of the Rotary, they

cooled. They were also horrified at the length of the papers I produced. They maintained that a one and a half page letter sufficed for the sale of preferred stock to the French. Fortunately, I realized that there was a big dispute about the meaning of the letter, and successfully maintained that there was a good deal to be said about the one-hundred page indenture. On the other hand, the English were much more friendly, entertaining us in London—and for country weekends.

Another very interesting case was one against the National Cash Register Company brought by a Dutch concern. It was in the French Civil Courts, but the Judge understood English quite well. I produced a monumental brief in English and ended up arguing the case for the Cash Register Company with my own French lawyer and the other side's standing by. The case was a very complicated one, but the Judge finally decided most of the points in my favor.

I also had an amusing but difficult time organizing Coca-Cola companies in Europe, traveling to Amsterdam and Luxembourg in the process. The leading Dutch bank refused to supply incorporation papers, and I was forced to use the Vatican brokerage firm, the only one willing to do it. On one of these train trips to Amsterdam, I played chess and won against a Russian lawyer, who had beaten Capablanca. To be sure, the master had been playing twenty boards at once, and when the Russian played me, he had a headache, but it was something to boast about, even though, I have to admit, he had given me his queen as a handicap.

Another job was the Guggenhein-inspired merger and international financing of the Nitrate companies in Chile. It was a tremendous operation, involving Robert G. Page, who was the Root Clark lawyer in Chile, who became a partner of mine some five years later. The longest cable probably ever sent, the by-laws, went off to Page from me. There was also an Anglo-American financing in London. It was quite good fun, drafting agreements in the English fashion with no punctuation. It made one realize how dependent we are on commas and the like. The sad thing was that the Compania de Salitre de Chile went into liquidation about a year afterwards, ruined by the artificial nitrate companies which sprang up all over Europe as a precursor of World War II.

When we returned to New York in 1931, I became involved in a spate of railroad reorganizations involving the Wabash and several trips to St. Louis with Arthur Gammell, a contentious Milbank Tweed partner, who eventually became quite a good friend and nominated me as executor of his will. The work was for a protective committee headed by the principal Vice President of the Prudential Life Insurance Company, who, one day, asked me for lunch and offered me the job of assistant solicitor of the Prudential at the then princely salary of $18,000. I was sorely tempted but finally turned him down, saying I wanted to stay in New York. He then asked me to suggest someone else. I recommended a fellow lawyer at Root Clark, Carrol M. Shanks, who accepted the job and steadily advanced to become an outstanding President. He was responsible for the Prudential policy of placing enormous regional offices in various cities and in overtaking Metropolitan primacy.

My first non-French litigation was an anti-trust case for the National Cash Register Company, which had to get Federal approval of a takeover of the Remington Cash Register Company. The case was tried by Emory Buckner in Columbus, Ohio, who left the entire preparation to me and an even younger fellow and read the brief for the first time on the train going out. The Court decided in our favor off the bench, excoriating the Department of Justice for opposing the merger. Afterwards, the court reporter came up to me and asked what the funny word was that Buckner had used. I said 'hege*mo*ny' and that Buckner had mispronounced it. He must have overheard me, as on our return to New York, he called me into his office. He had on his desk a large Webster's International Dictionary and asked me to look up the spelling of hegemony. I found to my distress that Buckner was absolutely right. It was he*ge*mony—my pronunciation came in third!

After two years back in New York, Root Clark, then regional counsel for the Reconstruction Finance Corporation, was asked in August of 1932 to lend me to them, as I had been doing some work for the New York Agency. So, down I went to Washington. Morton Bogue, a well-known New York lawyer, was General Counsel of the RFC. However, in December he announced his resignation and, astonishingly, recommended me as his successor. The Board of Directors actually elected me in the absence of Jesse Jones, a Democratic tycoon from Houston, who came back and insisted that someone more mature and more Democratic than I should be elected. He recommended Stanley Reed from the A.A.A.*, who was duly elected, and I was thrown a bone in the shape of the General Solicitorship. Reed and I got along beautifully. He cheerily let me handle the self-liquidating projects, the railroad loans and the financing of the banks. I certainly did not begrudge his later Solicitor Generalship of the U.S., nor his membership on the Supreme Court. For two weeks during the bank holiday, I was seconded to the Treasury Department, where I signed hundreds of telegrams "W. H. Woodin, Secretary of the Treasury," permitting or not permitting banks to reopen.

We made our first visit to the White House at this time. when my brother-in-law, Amyas Ames and his wife were visiting James Roosevelt there, the oldest son of the President. We were invited to an Easter Sunday lunch in the family dining room with only Louis Howe and his young daughter in addition. We were the guests of honor, and I remember sitting beside Mrs. Roosevelt, while my Boston wife sat on the President's right and was taking him to task for considering Mayor Curley as our first ambassador to the Vatican. As subsequently Curley was not appointed, she was convinced she might have had some effect.

After lunch, we decided it would be fun to go out on the Potomac in the Presidential yacht, the "Sequoia." This proved impossible on that particular Sunday, but in a large black limousine, the five of us (Betsy Roosevelt, Jimmy's wife was not there) headed instead for the Folger Shakespeare Library, built and managed by the Trustees of Amherst College, which none of us had seen. The Library, of course, was closed. Jimmy Roosevelt went up to the guard at the door and explained that his father was the President

---

*Agricultural Adjustment Administration.

of the United States and wouldn't he make an exception
and open the Library for us. He was refused firmly. Then
I spoke up and introduced myself, saying, "My father is
George A. Plimpton, President of the Board of Trustees of
Amherst College." The guard at once changed his expres-
sion and let us in!

It was while he was still in the Reconstruction Finance Corporation
that Francis wrote one of his first speeches, entitled "Law as a Career."
It was given at the Phillips Exeter Academy and subsequently published
in The Exeter Monthly for March, 1933. The Law was obviously a
profession in which he found satisfaction, despite its demands. He
certainly was committed to going back to it. The following article gives
his thoughts on this profession with the boys at Exeter in mind.

Law As A Career, 1933

It used to be a simple world. A bank was a place where you took large silver dollars, and the banker kept a good many of them, and lent some of them to your next door neighbor to build a barn. Shoes were made by the shoemaker and the hoe factory had fifty hands, bought iron from second cousins in Pennsylvania, and sold the hoes over most of the country.

That has all changed, so much changed that most of us go through life without ever fully understanding the complex interplay of economic and social institutions and forces which make us rich or poor, contented or depressed.

A lawyer has changed with his changing world. He used to argue, oratorically or saltily, before juries whom he knew and who knew him, about boundary lines and cows, libels in the county seat weekly gazette, contracts for the sale of the back pasture. He foreclosed a few mortgages, drew simple wills, settled small estates, dabbled expertly in politics, drove a shrewd bargain in horseflesh. It was not out of the question for him to know about all the law there was to know; success came not so much from book learning or thorough analysis of complicated problems as from knowledge of human nature and aptness in the art of dealing with men.

The lawyer of the present is a different animal, almost a different species. He tends primarily, in a world of specialists, to be a specialist himself. Today no lawyer could possibly dream of attempting to know all the law there is to know. He is buried in an avalanche of statutes from

Congress and the forty-eight states, ordinances from every
city and town, regulations and rulings from a legion of
public utility commissions, tax departments and other administrative boards and bureaus; he is drowned in a cascade
of published decisions from ninety-seven federal courts (not
including offshoots such as the Court of Claims and the
United States Court for China) and innumerable state courts,
from attorney generals, from the Interstate Commerce Commission, the Federal Trade Commission, the Board of Tax
Appeals and other special tribunals. The watches of the night
bring to many a modern lawyer the sinking feeling that the
stuff of the law, from which he must fashion decisions
affecting life and happiness and property, has grown too
bulky and tangled for the human hand to handle.

It is the fashion to blame legislatures and courts for the
engulfing tide of the law. As well blame them because we
no longer spin our own wool, because a freight rate from
Albany to Boston may spell poverty to a North Dakota
farmer and Liverpool shipowner, or because one hundred
thousand humans live in one square mile. One may criticize
the channels, or the choice of them, through which the law
is expanding, but it is as futile to yearn for a simple body
of law in a complicated world as it is to raise your own
vegetables in a Manhattan apartment. One cannot accept
the benefits, such as they are, of a highly specialized economic order, networked with a veritable nervous system of
interrelations and interdependencies, without at the same
time inevitably submitting to a greater and more complex
social control through law.

Not only has the present day lawyer to deal with a
massive and intricate system of law, made so by the society
which conditions it and which it conditions, but the non-
legal raw material of his problems has become increasingly
harder to master.

A murder case is still a murder case—though counsel
must now be quasi-experts in fingerprinting, ballistics and
dementia praecox. But it is a far cry from foreclosing the
mortgage on the back pasture to reorganizing a railroad,
which starts with the foreclosure of a one hundred and fifty
page mortgage and involves the conflicting legal and finan-

cial claims of as many as a dozen different classes of creditors and stockholders. There are still thousands of lawsuits where the sole issue is whether the plaintiff is an injured martyr or an inveterate liar, but there are thousands of others where the lawyers must temporarily become certified public accountants, or electrical engineers, or dress designers, in order to know what it is all about.

The same is even more true of legal work at the junction points between the law and business. This type of legal work, increasingly important because of the increasing importance of law to business, involves assisting in the formation of business and financial policies within the limitations permitted by law, and the carrying out of such policies through the legal mechanisms of corporations and contracts. Obviously no lawyers can do such work effectively without being thoroughly familiar with the business and financial problems involved.

The modern lawyer then is a specialist, an expert, and must be prepared to dig down into problems the legal and practical roots of which are often a matted and intertwined mass of technical details.

I am of course exaggerating, and am confessedly writing from the viewpoint of the big city legal specialist. There are literally tens of thousands of lawyers whose work today is no more specialized and no more difficult than it would have been fifty years ago. But I think I am right as to the trend, and the trend is something which is of distinct importance to those who are wondering whether the law is the career for them.

What are the implications? It seems to me that there are at least two.

The first is that, in general, no man is likely to be a successful lawyer today unless he has a first class brain. You are all used to being told, by parents and wandering alumni, that a *cum laude* or a Phi Beta Kappa key is more important in later life than a football letter. I do not pretend to know whether such a generalization is true in its entirety; but I do know that your law school scholastic ranking (and it's fairly likely to follow what you've done in school and college) will have a definite dollars and cents effect on your chances of getting a good job and of getting well paid for it. Personality may help, but it is brains that count. Marks are not an unfailing index of brains, but unless you get pretty good marks don't try to be a lawyer. You may succeed, but the chances are against you.

The second implication is that the mind of the present day lawyer must be rugged enough to work at top speed for twelve or more hours a day and tough enough to enjoy battling with stubborn facts and complicated legal problems. Don't try to be a lawyer unless you like hard work and unless you are spurred on—not turned aside—by the challenge of difficulty.

If you are going to be a lawyer, choose hard courses in school and college. Concentrate on political science, economics, subjects that are hard and that relate to the world that you're going to practice law in. Don't neglect Latin, mathematics, subjects that are hard and are good for your mind because they are hard. Go to a good law school and work your head off. Remember that your success is going to depend largely on your brain—exercise it, give it hard jobs to do and make it work.

I am afraid that I have drawn rather a forbidding picture of the law as a career, and probably an exaggerated one. We all know that not every successful lawyer is a mental giant who rejoices in hair cloth shirts and revels in working eighteen hours a day on problems so difficult and technical that no one else can understand them. But it is a hard profession, and there's no getting away from it.

The rewards? There are a good many. From the purely material point of view, legal ability commands a good price in its own field. In addition, first class lawyers are constantly being asked to step across the border line (sometimes indistinct, anyway) between law and business or finance into positions of high responsibility and worldly remuneration. A complicated world will always pay tribute to a man who understands complexities.

The law is one of the natural pathways to public service. In spite of the encroachment of business upon the law (or, if you prefer, the encroachment of law upon business), the lawyer still remains a professional man, a servant of the system of justice. Proverbially he can use the law as a stepping stone into politics or governmental service, and private practice itself often stimulates the high exaltation that comes with a fight for a just principle or a just cause.

The law provides its own intellectual return. If you have that quality Thorstein Veblen called the instinct of workmanship, the inner urge for a hard job well done, the law will satisfy all the cravings of your spirit and will delight your soul.

I have never understood why the law should be personified by so essentially illegal an individual as a mistress. But if she is a mistress, and a jealous one, she is also endlessly challenging and fascinating and, on the whole, not a bad person to go through life with.

● ● ●

Forty-six years later, at the Commencement of the Vermont Law School Class of 1979, an occasion upon which he received the honorary degree of L.L.D., Francis gave a second address entitled "The Law As A Career"—this time reflections based on four decades of law practice.

Law As A Career, 1979

There are a good many reasons why I am delighted to be here today.

First, Mr. Chairman*, your Honor, is the honor of being presided over by you, my law school classmate. You are a member of a court, the Court of Appeals for the Second Circuit, which is properly recognized by all Vermonters (and by all New Yorkers and Connecticuters) as the best court, bar none, in the United States. Warping slightly a story told by Paul Freund of the time when he was Mr. Justice Brandeis' law clerk, he said that the Brandeis opinions overruling lower courts always ended "reversed and remanded for proceedings consistent with this opinion," except that, in the very rare case of a reversal of the Court of Appeals for the Second Circuit, they always read "reversed and remanded for proceedings not inconsistent with this opinion."

My second reason for my pleasure at being here is to be able to tell a Debevoise story. This one is not about Dean Debevoise, but is told about and by his father, Eli Whitney Debevoise, Sterry Waterman's and my law school classmate, my dear friend for 46 years and my dear partner for almost 37—to my great regret he cannot be here today. While Whitney was in Law School he married a charming Radcliffe undergraduate. They put off their honeymoon for more than a year, and then went to France for the summer, where they stayed in a Paris pension presided over by a

---

*Sterry Waterman, senior judge for the Second Circuit and Chairman of the Board of Trustees.

very motherly landlady. She asked how long they had been married. When he said a little over a year, she said, "Oh, a year, and still no little one?" He explained, "Well, you see, my wife hadn't finished her course at Radcliffe." The landlady said, "Oh, in the United States you must take a course for that too?"

My third reason for liking to be here is to pay tribute to Thomas Debevoise and what I can't help thinking of as his Law School. He is a prime example of what deToqueville admired in the American character some 150 years ago, the pragmatic spirit of sturdily doing it yourself. Someone sees a need, a lack, something that is missing. No law school in Vermont? Tommy didn't run to the State, or the University of Vermont, or Washington, or anywhere else. He did something about it himself, and within four years, with the help of a distinguished and dedicated Board of Trustees, a full-fledged Law School had been born, with a first class faculty and a student body from more than 150 colleges spread across the country—surely an unparalleled achievement in legal education.

And now a few words to the 1979 product of that Law School.

One thing you don't need to worry about is jobs. Orders for durable goods may be 12% less than they were a year ago, but the production of statutes, laws, boards, commissions, administrations, agencies, rules, regulations, interpretations, opinions and rulings is the fastest growing industry in the United States, and whether the public likes it or not (and it doesn't like it), the need for lawyers is greater than ever and is going to get even greater. All of this year's J.D.'s and thousands of others could profitably be turned loose on the 352 pages of the Tax Reform Act of 1969, the 581 pages of the Tax Reform Act of 1976, the 56 pages of the Revenue Act of 1978 and whatever simplifications (sure to be monstrously complicated) may be in store for us. And if that bonanza for the profession, the Equal Rights Amendment, should ever be ratified, we will all have to spend the next 50 years in construing it. I am sure that none of you is under any illusion that your J.D.'s constitute a legal education—they are just a beginning. You have only to look at the courses in law school you didn't take, or at the vast sweep of the law beyond academic horizons or at the relentless march of new developments in the law and its institutions. Less than 50 years ago there were whole areas which were little touched by the law, but are now increasingly tangled in legal complexities—securities, labor relations, wages and hours, pensions, safety, health, environment, civil rights, equal rights, fair employment and what not. Who will say that there will not be increasingly changing law in those areas and in areas yet to come?

What this means is that to keep abreast of your profession you must *keep* learning. Continuing legal education is not a luxury but a necessity. Indeed, several states actually require that a lawyer, to remain in good standing, must take a prescribed amount of legal education each year.

Another challenge you must face is the growing demand for effective legal services for all. The jibe that the courts of justice, like the Ritz Hotel, are open to rich and poor alike, can no longer be tolerated. The disadvantaged must get the legal services they need and deserve. The federal Legal Services Corporation will help and it is right that it should—after all, the federal government subsidizes wheat, corn, tobacco (while the Surgeon General denounces smoking), AMTRAK, housing and health care, why not legal services? We should cooperate with the Corporation and support the local Legal Aid Society, but, more importantly, we should give of ourselves.

The House of Delegates of the American Bar Association has unanimously resolved that it is the official duty of every practicing lawyer to provide public interest legal service, meaning work done without a fee or at a substantially reduced fee, in poverty law, civil rights law, public rights law (i.e. representing an important right belonging to a significant part of the public), work for charitable organizations or work toward the improvement of justice. I suppose there is hardly any lawyer who does not have a slightly guilty feeling (mine is more than slight) that he has not fully lived up to those responsibilities. As a matter of fact, there is serious discussion in certain bar association circles, and possibly in legislative circles as well, that these pro bono responsibilities should be made legal requirements. Heaven forfend that we get snarled up in any such entanglements; let us see to it that our fulfillment of those responsibilities makes any such regulation unnecessary.

You are entering a profession in ferment.

We always used to think that we *were* a profession, but now the Supreme Court tells us that we are a trade and that the time honored prohibition against advertising is a restraint of trade, and that fee schedules are a restraint of trade. It will do us no good to bewail the possible commercialization of the practice of law—the Court was thinking about the good of the public, and we should be too. The public *is* entitled to more information about lawyers and what they can and can't do, and *is* entitled to the benefits of competition. We must expand our referral services, develop the certification of specialists so that the public will know what to look for, make sure of our own competence by continuing legal education, and let the public know what we are up to by modest and accurate advertising consistent with our self-respect.

I suppose that every lawyer since the days of Hammurabi has maintained that never before in history has law been subject to such stress as at the then moment, but I must say that we have a very strong case for our own times and the times to come.

I hope that you J.D.'s of the class of 1979, and all the rest of us, may really feel those necessities and that all of us may respond to that challenge in the high tradition of dedicated services for which we like to think our profession has always stood.

● ● ●

In the Fall of 1933, Francis resigned from the R.F.C. and we went back to New York and that "jealous mistress." Our year and a half in Washington for the R.F.C. had been a broadening experience. It was an exciting time, as Francis felt that he was helping to rescue the country from the Depression and was taking part in the innovative changes that the new Administration brought. However, at this point, he had begun to dream of starting his own firm. To continue in his words:

After considering several possibilities, I ended up join-
ing Eli Whitney Debevoise and William E. Stevenson, who
had started out courageously nearly two years earlier, both
coming out of Davis Polk. Whitney Debevoise, a Yale man,
was a classmate of mine at Harvard Law School. I also
knew Bill Stevenson. When I was manager of the Exeter
track team and Bill was captain of the Andover track team,
I went on a pilgrimage to Andover organized by the Chris-
tian Fraternity of Exeter, of which I happened to be Vice
President. I was received and ushered around Andover by
Bill Stevenson, who was a famous runner there as well as
at Princeton and Oxford where he took his law degree as a
Rhodes Scholar. I had great admiration for both of them
and had no difficulty in deciding to join their new Firm.
The Firm became Debevoise, Stevenson and Plimpton in
1933.

One of the first things that happened after I joined the
Firm was an offer from Norman H. Davis, Roosevelt's first
Ambassador at Large and the head of the U.S. delegation
to the Disarmament Conference in Geneva, asking me to
act as his personal counsel in connection with his recent
designation to try to clean up the Kreuger and Toll Match
Co. collapse in Stockholm.

He called me over to his office on a Friday morning and
suggested that I confer with Allen Dulles, who was his
disarmament advisor and who had previously declined the
Kreuger and Toll offer. Accordingly, I went that afternoon
and talked to Allen, an old friend. On Monday morning I
went to see Mr. Davis, who embarrassedly said that Allen
had just refused to continue as disarmament advisor if he
weren't given the addition of the Kreuger and Toll coun-
selship. Mr. Davis further said that Allen Dulles' disarmament connection was so important that he regretfully and
even more embarrassedly withdrew the offer of the Kreuger
and Toll job!

This was not the last contretemps that I had with the
Dulles brothers. An impecunious investor dropped in about
this time to ask us to contest, on a contingency fee basis,
the National Investors merger. I spent an hour talking to
Foster Dulles and his partner Rogers Lamont, both for the

merger. It was obviously a very complicated matter, and I said I would get in touch with them if we decided to act.

The Firm decided not to take the case. Several months later, I ran into John Burns, then the General Counsel of the S.E.C., who immediately asked why my Firm had approved the merger, saying that Foster Dulles in his argument before the full Commission had used the fact that we had approved the merger as his primary argument. A completely false statement!

The Firm went through various metamorphoses since those early beginning days. Robert A. Page of Root Clark joined in 1936, later to leave to help head Phelps Dodge. Then the Firm almost collapsed during the War as partners and young lawyers departed for war service. Stevenson went off to head the American Red Cross in Europe. Later, he became President of Oberlin, Ambassador to the Philippines and Chairman of the Aspen Institute for Humanistic Studies. Debevoise became Chairman of Draft Regulation in New York. I was asked to go to London as civilian counsel of the Eighth Air Force to make suggestions to improve its capabilities. However, besides having four children and wanting to preserve what was left of the Firm, I had agreed with Debevoise that neither would leave. So, after much anguish, I refused.

In 1943, the war was in full swing and Amherst college had only about twenty seniors graduating. The College was predominately training four or five hundred youngsters for combat duty in France. We visited a class of high school boys being taught French by a professor, called a "chatterer," preparing them to be dropped by parachute behind the line on D-day—a sobering experience. Stanley King, the President, as an economy measure, prudently asked one of the Trustees to give the Commencement Address. This was the result.

The Fifth Freedom

I suggest that we consider this afternoon the fifth freedom—the freedom of the mind.

This is the basic freedom, the indispensable inner freedom from which the other freedoms must spring if they are to be anything except empty symbols. Freedom of speech, freedom of religion—both of them are meaningless unless the speech and the religion come from a mind that is free, and freedom from want and freedom from fear offer nothing but animal satisfactions if they are not at the service of a free mind.

The worst thing that Hitler has done is not the beheading of those who speak against him, or the suffocation of religion, or the use of want and fear as weapons of terror with which to club human beings into abject submission. His vilest sin is that he has enslaved and degraded men's minds.

I wonder how many of you have actually read "Mein Kampf", that strange and turgid testament of a warped genius—yes, genius—whose emotional epileptic force has surged over all Europe in ten years. There is an underlying motif in that book, his hatred of the free mind. The bitterest vials of his contempt are poured over the intellectual process, the thinking of free men. To Hitler, the function of the human mind is to wear a brown shirt in the service of the leader, to obey orders, to do what it is told. Thought is stamped with the swastika and thrust into the forced labor battalions.

There has been no such studied attempt to tyrannize the

human mind since the Spanish Inquisition. For that dark chapter in history there was perhaps the excuse of ignorance, but for Hitler's contemptuous and snarling imprisonment of man's mind there is none.

It is peculiarly appropriate that the planes which fly deepest into the Third Reich should be called Liberators, for their ultimate mission is the liberation of the captive minds and bodies of those whom Hitler has brought to heel.

Nor must it be forgotten that Hitler is not the only one who has laid an iron hand on the freedom of the mind. The unsmiling and barbaric fanatics who rule Japan behind the mask of a dim-witted Emperor have long since brought down the curtain of night over the Japanese mind. In that oriental darkness, the forces that move are not the forces of mind and reason, but the lowering formless shapes of inscrutable violence and calculated death.

In a quiet grove of Cryptomeria, high above Kyoto, splashed with sunlight and shadow, the grave of Joseph Neesima, who graduated from this College in 1870, looks down at the university he founded to carry to that valley the things of the mind and the spirit he had found in this valley. I am afraid he sleeps a troubled sleep. It is not only that he hears of the cold murders of prisoners of war, he has heard the sentence of death passed on the freedom of the mind which he had brought from this College and nurtured with gentle patience for so many years before the shadows began to gather.

Nor, to keep our own thinking straight, must we forget our wholly hard-boiled comrade Joseph Stalin, who would smile faintly, with a touch of sardonic amusement, at the bizarre suggestion that the minds of the Russian people should be allowed to be completely free. For that matter, I imagine that there are plenty of Chinese, and North African French, Arabs and Jews, and South Americans, who could testify that despotism over the human mind is not the unique prerogative of Berlin, Tokyo, and Rome.

Indeed, to look at the splinters in our own eyes, the liberty of the mind is none too secure in this country. There are times when the Dies Committee seems to regard any mind to the left of right field as a mind to be suppressed,

and there are decisions of the National Labor Relations
Board which mean that the employees' minds are free to
go any way they want, but that the employer's mind can,
under penalty of the law, go only one way.

No one knows whether winning the war will mean the
winning of the fifth freedom, or of the other four, in this
country or in any other country. But one thing we do know,
and that is that *not* winning the war, winning it uncondi-
tionally, would mean that the darkness in Central Europe
and East Asia would overshadow our freedoms and our very
lives.

We may be uncertain what we are fighting for, but we
know what we are fighting *against*, and that is the fight we
are utterly and resolutely determined to win.

Now I am going to assume that we will win that fight,
and I am going to resist the not very strong temptation to
explore with you the whole problem of the fifth freedom in
the post war world. Instead, I should like to talk to you
members of the class of 1943 about the freedom of *your*
minds.

I do not know whether your minds are free now or not.
Minds are not created free, any more than they are created
equal. I can remember as if it were yesterday the first sentence in the first book on economics I ever studied in this
College:

"Men do not make communities—they
are born and bred into them."

So with our minds. They are born and bred into our sur-
roundings, and are formed and moulded by those surround-
ings. During the long years of family life and school life,
our minds are taking on substance and shape and color from
the people and things that surround us. There is no freedom,
there is no pleasant servitude to our families and to the
familiar concepts and traditions that are never questioned
because they are the very stuff from which our mental experience is slowly and unconsciously fashioned.

The first stirrings of the freedom of the mind come with
college. There are various stimuli that in college, for the
first time, energize the mind into the sense of its freedom
and power.

Perhaps it is the stimulus of one of those formulas that starts slowly and painfully in the upper left hand corner of the blackboard, descends majestically in a dignified and complicated procession of Arabic figures, Greek letters and cabalistic symbols, pauses for anxious reflection in a welter of sines, cosines, and radices, gathers momentum with a cascade of Cyrillic squiggles, and nose dives triumphantly, with the chalk squealing and the white dust flying, until the answer, beautiful in the perfection of its rightness, pours itself out into the lower right hand corner of the board.

Perhaps it is the stimulus of real translation from Latin or Greek or German or French, a translation that is accurate, that catches the very essence and flavor of the original, and recreates that essence and flavor into English that marches like the Latin, or sings like the Greek, or trudges sure-footedly like the German, or dances with the bright precision of the French.

Perhaps it is the stimulus of scientific experiment, the slow meticulous preparation, the checking, the verification of detail, the careful excision of the variables, the patient waiting, and finally the culmination of an hypothesis radiantly sustained.

Perhaps it is the stimulus of a fresh viewpoint on the institutions of man, seen for the first time from a variant angle and with a new glass; what were valleys in shadow are now valleys in light; the familiar contours suddenly stand out with arresting sharpness; unnoticed details leap into focus; the whole landscape of human institutions is vibrant with new and meaningful significance.

These are some of the stimuli, and there are many more of them, that you have had in this College. They are stimuli that should have given your minds that sense of exhilaration, of unleashing, of expansion, of unconquerable outpouring power, of the limitless horizons of the human spirit, that means that your minds have come of age and are free.

This College has given you those stimuli because it is a liberal college, a college of the freedom of the mind. No books have ever been burned on this campus, and you and the rest of us will see to it that none ever will be. No teacher on this faculty needs to swear allegiance to anyone or anything except the obligation to teach the truth and teach it well.

You should be proud of your College for the answer it has given to what attempts *have* been made to censor the freedom of its faculty. The answer has been given calmly, without self-advertising histrionics, and the answer has been "No".

You are now leaving the intellectual freedom of this College, and must guard, for yourselves, the freedom of your minds.

I do not believe that the freedom of your minds faces much of a threat in this country from *outside*. Americans do not like to be pushed around, by their government or by anyone else. We can be accused of many things, but never of docility. Whatever the reason may be, whether it is the historical heritage of the urge for freedom that led religious and economic minorities here from Europe, or the legacy of the revolution celebrated by that most anti-revolutionary of bodies, the Daughters of the American Revolution, or the influence of the frontier so dear to economic historians, or simply the thorough training in prohibition, Americans make very poor dictates.

This is true even in unexpected quarters. You all remember the old story, probably apocryphal, told of Cardinal Gibbons during the excitement, a good many years ago, about an encyclical which reasserted the infallibility of the Pope. The Cardinal had just returned to this country from an audience with the Pope in Rome, and was asked by a brash reporter whether, as a result of that audience, he believed in the Pope's infallibility. The Cardinal cocked an eye, and replied, "Well, he called me *J*ibbons!"

The danger to the freedom of your minds will not come, I think, from without, but from *within*.

No emancipation proclamation can make your minds forever free; you will have to enforce your own Thirteenth Amendment.

In your fight for the freedom of your minds you have had, in this College, the advantage of good teaching; from now on you must rely on good learning.

You will have to learn the moral of the old story of the

successful negro shopkeeper, who was asked how he had done so well. He replied, "I ain't had no education—I had to use my brains."

One of the dangers from within that you must guard yourself against is the danger of singleness of mind.

All down the ages men have tried to explain and interpret the world in terms of one single approach, one single element.

The Greek philosophers quarreled among themselves as to what that single element was; one thought it was fire, another air, another water; Pythagoras was sure that it was numbers; Heraclitus that it was flux and change.

The medieval scholiasts explained everthing in terms of the will of God. The scientists of the middle ages spent their time searching for the touchstone, the one omnipotent element which was to be the master of all others.

I do not know what the answer to the riddle of the universe is, but I do know that there is not one riddle but many riddles, and that there is not one answer but many answers. Knowledge is a seamless web, and you can't tear off part of it and wave it as a banner, and think that you are conquering in the struggle for the truth.

I suspect that the time has come for the kingdoms of the world to make a Declaration of Interdependence; I am even more sure that the time has come for the provinces of the mind to make a Declaration of Interdependence. That Declaration means that no single banner can possibly lead the forces of your mind to truth.

You must not underestimate the threat to the freedom of your minds that comes from the yearning for simplicity, for one single explanation, one single motif, one touchstone for the problems of the mind.

You must resolutely set your strength against that yearning, for if you give in, if you accept one hypothesis, one approach, one viewpoint, one interpretation, one answer, your minds will be chained in a concentration camp of your own contriving.

This is not a monistic world, it is a pluralistic world, and you must face it as it is. You must face diversity, you must face pluralism. You must accept their challenge, and make your minds self-reliant and tough and preserving and realistic enough not to surrender to singleness of formula but to fight on through to disparate, *ad hoc*, thinking analyses of the particular facts, illuminated by no one colored lamp but only by the clear light of the free mind, a white light—for white is the fusion of all colors.

A further danger to the freedom of your minds is the danger of difficulty.

All of us wonder why German minds succumbed so completely to authoritarianism, to totalitarianism. I think we tend to forget how tempting it is to surrender the freedom of the mind. Difficulties and complexities mount, and those who tire of the rigorous and never-ending effort of free thinking find a certain soft spurious relief in giving up the struggle and sinking down to rest in the delusive ease of dependence of mind.

Independence of mind, on the other hand, is difficult. It is a hard thing to be free, and not to turn to another mind for the answers. You will all remember the little girl who, after a week or so of a progressive school, came up to her teacher in the morning and said, "Teacher, this morning do we *have* to do what we want to do?"

A few weeks ago, in the Low Library at Columbia, I was looking at a fifteenth century manuscript called the "Margarita Philosophica", in a collection given by a graduate of this College.* It is a compendium of just about all the knowledge that there was in the world in the middle fourteen hundreds. The manuscript is perhaps an inch and a half thick. The compendium of today's knowledge which the Messrs. Sears, Roebuck & Co. produce under the name "Encyclopedia Britannica" runs to 28 volumes, not to mention a fat appendix each year.

That is symbolic of the growing weight of the sheer facts of this world, which, if you do not look out, will crush the freedom of your minds by their very mass. You will need all your courage and strength to fend off some of those facts, and bear up under others, and assimilate and master those facts (no matter how many or how difficult) that concern you and your thinking.

I have warned you against the danger of knowing only

---

*George Arthur Plimpton

one answer; just as bad a danger is being discouraged by difficulty into not knowing any answers at all. You face the eternal dilemma; to be free, your minds must be deep but not narrow, and broad but not shallow.

You are now leaving this place of the freedom of the mind, this pleasant hill, that square white tower that rises above the mounting trees and looks out at the Pelham Hills.

As you go, I want you to remember the seal of your College. It is a simple seal, with nothing on it except a shining sun, free and open to all, and an open book, free and open to all. Underneath is the phrase "Terras irradient", let that sun and that open book give light to the lands of the world.

May you, with free minds, yourselves give light to the lands where you go.

●   ●   ●

To return to Francis' account of his legal career:

I remained all through the War in New York and when Debevoise went to Germany as a counsel for John J. McCloy, then High Commissioner, I was the head of the Firm for a year. As time went on, various partners were added. Edward C. McLean, who was a classmate of Alger Hiss and represented him in the first trial and who later left to become a Federal Judge, Marvin Lyons, a tax authority from Davis Polk, and Samuel E. Gates, an aviation and litigation specialist, up from a Washington firm, all joined. The Firm for many years was known as Debevoise, Plimpton, Lyons & Gates until 1981, when it became Debevoise & Plimpton, the two remaining senior partners.

During the Depression years and the War that followed, there were few new law firms being established. We were fortunate in attracting a very good group of young lawyers, who chose our Firm because they saw more chance for advancement than they would have had in the older established firms. As a result, the Firm acquired an increasingly good reputation, and I was proud of the way it developed. I remember back to some of the highlights of my part in it.

I worked in the corporation field, starting with the Allied Owners reorganization, representing the RFC, which insisted on everyone working for ten dollars an hour. Debevoise successfully argued the case on appeal to the Supreme Court. I had a very early registration under the Securities Act of 1933 (South Western Bell Telephone Bonds). Then I won a holding that the Hungarian Exchange Controls governed the Hungarian Bank of Pest, and was very pleased at reversing Surrogate Foley's (a great Irish Democrat) construction of a will which I argued on appeal against Samuel Seabury. I had a series of railroad reorganizations—the Florida East Coast with trips to Jacksonville, which went on for seventeen years and involved the first disaffirmance of an Equipment Trust in modern times. I found myself buying railroad locomotives, freight cars and cabooses and subsequently peddling them out to other railroads; the Norfolk Southern, trips to Norfolk; the Central of Georgia, trips to Savannah (quail shooting in a Chesterfield overcoat); the Erie utilities corporations, General Gas and Electric and American Power and Light and then a whole series of private placements for insurance companies interspersed with estates and cases coming from international connections.

●   ●   ●

The firm of Debevoise, Plimpton, Lyons & Gates flourished and grew. When Francis joined the firm in 1933, it was composed of the three partners and two associate lawyers—now there are two hundred and twelve lawyers, including sixty-four partners.

Francis was always so modest about his law career that I am going to paraphrase Geoffrey Hellman on the subject, from his "New Yorker" profile called "Period-Piece Fellow" (December 4, 1971):

He is known as an unrivalled drawer-up of indentures— sealed contracts between two or more parties, with mutual covenants that call for an arcane, highly technical form of composition. Plimpton's pioneering in this field is generally recognized in legal circles. "He has de-James Joyced the indenture," a colleague has said, and William L. Cary, a former S.E.C. chairman who now teaches law at Columbia, has included an appendix of Plimpton legal drafts in "Cases and Materials on Corporations," a casebook on corporate law and finance that has been used in ninety law schools. "Francis provided me with a model around which discussion could play," Professor Cary has said of this book. "He's the only person who can write an indenture in iambic pentameter." . . . Indentures . . . constitute . . . the cornerstone of Plimpton's legal career . . .

The life of a lawyer goes on with a certain placidity. We lived in a top apartment at 1165 Fifth Avenue at Ninety-Eighth Street, with a view over the Reservoir and the East River. It was given us by Francis's father, who insisted that his grandchildren should grow up in as much sunlight as New York could offer. We brought up our four children in this pleasant environment, spending summers and weekends on Long Island, where the beauty of the seasons flowed on each year from forsythia to dogwood and azaleas, to laurel and red roses, to day lilies. Exercise was an essential element in Francis' life. He especially enjoyed golf, tennis and squash. When he didn't have a game, he ran around the Reservoir in Central Park or our meadow in the country. In our early days in Paris, he ran laps around the Champs de Mars and startled the French by organizing touch-football games in the Bois de Boulogne. He had the pleasure of playing with his sons in men's doubles in both tennis and squash. Our three sons and our daughter Sarah, the youngest, grew up and went to school and college and the boys to the Armed Services, with the usual problems and triumphs and then went their several ways. Always there was the Long Island Railroad with the daily commuting in summer and the waiting wives at the Cold Spring Harbor station. Then, in the fall of 1960, the complacency of our lives was changed.

PART TWO

Diplomacy

Diplomacy

In 1961 we were catapulted into the world of diplomacy. Adlai Stevenson had been a roommate of Francis during his second year at Harvard Law School and had been a close friend ever since. They had been assistant Sergeants at Arms together at the Democratic National Convention in 1924. Adlai stayed with Francis at his father's house in Murray Hill. We had kept in touch, visiting him in Lake Geneva, outside of Chicago, when he became engaged to Ellen Borden; we had seen the Stevensons often in Washington, when Adlai was working for the Agricultural Adjustment Administration and with the Secretary of the Navy, Frank Knox. We would go out to his famous birthday parties, which were celebrated with festivities and the wit, humor and gaiety Adlai would bring to such occasions. His friends would come from far and near, and there would be entertainment, such as a magician to read our minds or an act from Chicago's "Second City." Francis himself read a poem at one of them. The first year that Adlai was Ambassador to the United Nations, living at 42A in the Waldorf Astoria (he brought his own housekeeper with him from Libertyville), his friends gave him a kitchen shower!

Our friendship also led us into adventures. Stevenson was in the habit of inviting friends to travel with him to distant countries of the world. We made our first trip with him along with the Hermon Dunlap Smiths and William McCormick Blair of Chicago to Alaska, after he had lost the 1954 election and was making appearances to help raise money for the Democratic Party.

We went up the Inland Passageway by steamer, a marvelous sight, everything in grays and whites with occasional small turquoise icebergs. We were met and escorted to every city. Flying in single engine planes, we flew low over mountains with active glaciers and far north over the tundra and herds of reindeer and elk. The farthest north we went was Kotzebue, a small Eskimo village with *six* churches built by different denominations. In Kotzebue, Adlai was tossed in an Eskimo blanket.

Our second trip with Adlai was in 1959 through the Mediterranean as guests of William Benton, who had chartered The Flying Clipper, a Swedish training ship with cadets as crew. It was three-masted, one mast square rigged, huge (195 feet), and resembled a pirate ship. Among the guests (we boarded at Valencia) were Roger Stevens, George Ball, young Adlai III with his wife, and Marietta Tree. Again, we were met and entertained to a state of exhaustion. Only Adlai seemed to be able to stand it. I can still see him at a bull fight, sitting beside the Mayor of the town shouting with more verve than anyone, "Olé, Olé!"

We sailed to Majorca, visited Robert Graves, who gave us lemonade and local gin and tried to persuade us that Columbus had originally sailed from Majorca. Then, setting all sails, on to Manorca and then Corsica where we entered the most dramatic harbor I have ever seen, Bonifacio. It is so narrow with high cliffs on either side that maneuvering the huge vessel in was quite a feat. We left with Adlai the next morning, after being entertained with dances in the evening. We were piped ashore, the sailors in white uniforms, oars held upright as we boarded and then rowing in rhythm.

During these travels, Francis and Adlai came to know each other very well, so that it was not surprising when Adlai was appointed Ambassador to the United Nations by President John F. Kennedy, that he called on Francis to ask him to be his number two man in the U.S. Mission. The President had given Adlai a free hand in making appointments to the Mission. The political spectrum of Francis was wide and would have startled the Senate Committee, if not the President, if he had been grilled on it. Francis was actually an Independent, having voted for such losing candidates as La Follette and Al Smith. He happened to be registered as a Republican in Suffolk County, Long Island. However, he was appointed by President Kennedy and sailed through the Senate Committee, chaired by Senator William Fulbright because, as he remembered, they were more interested in the man preceding him before the Committee, George Kennan, who had been appointed Ambassador to Yugoslavia. Thus suddenly, Francis, straight out of the private sector, became an Ambassador Extraordinary and Plenipotentiary, actually the same rank as Stevenson's. We went down to the White House to the reception for the Presidential appointees. It was an impressive ceremony. As we went down the line to shake hands, both the President and Jackie in turn asked, "How's George!"*

Francis was involved at once in the turmoil and excitement of the United Nations, always very grateful to the young career diplomats in the Mission who guided him in the beginning. Francis was the Deputy Representative of the U.S. in the Security Council and served as the U.S. Representative on the Special Committee, the Legal Committee (the sixth) and occasionally the Budget Committee (the fifth). He was a member of the U.S. Delegation to the 15th–19th U.N. General Assemblies. He particularly enjoyed being the U.S. Representative on the Special Committee on the Peaceful Uses of Outer Space. On one occasion he took the whole Committee down to Cape Canaveral to inspect the installation of our space program there. One of the incidents while he served on this committee is described by Richard Gardner in Geoffrey Hellman's "New Yorker" article on Francis.

Professor Gardner said:

> I was his deputy on the U.N. Committee on the Peaceful Uses of Outer Space, on which he was the U.S. representative. That was a success story—one of the few solid U.N. accomplishments in the sixties. We got a space treaty—no nuclear weapons on celestial bodies or in space, no claims of sovereignty—and a world weather watch. Francis bears a great deal of credit for all that. One of the problems was the question of liability for things shot into space by one country that fell down in another country. There were, of course, really only two countries that *shot* things into space. Well, one day at a Committee meeting Francis produced a large fragment of a Soviet sputnik that had fallen, smoking hot, from the heavens into a street in Manitowoc, Wisconsin. He dropped this hugh metal lump in front of the Soviet desk. "Here, gentlemen," he said. It was one of his finest hours.
>
> Plimpton himself says of the episode, "I produced this thing the size of a football at a time when the United States was pressing for an international agreement on liability for accidents originating in outer space. I asked my Soviet counterpart to come and get it. He looked at it as though it were

---

*George Plimpton, our eldest son, a friend of both.

a viper." (In his oral history, Plimpton technically and her-
petologically amplified this account: "We knew it was from
a Soviet vehicle because it contained part of a screw, and
the screw-thread intervals were measurable in millimeters,
and not in fractions of an inch—clear proof that it was of
Soviet manufacture. I publicly offered to give it to Morozov
[his Russian counterpart], who shrank away as if it were a
puff adder. After the furor died down, some days later, he
did come around and ask to have it.")

Another incident was the question of Outer Mongolia and Mauritania. To quote from his oral history (for the John F. Kennedy Library,
1969):

I remember my anguish at having to explain in my
somewhat battered French the position of the United States
to the French-speaking Africans. It came down to this: the
Africans were all very anxious to get Mauritania into the
U.N., and the Soviets would veto it unless Outer Mongolia
came in. I had the nice little job of trying to persuade
China—Taiwan—not to veto Outer Mongolia, which they
regard as part of China. You get curious crossruffs there.
It's a mild revelation when you get into U.N. affairs to
realize how terrifically political a lot of these issues are. It's
no question of right or wrong; it's just a question of straight
political muscle. Well, we finally exercised our political
muscle on Taiwan and made them agree to let Mongolia in,
which they could have blocked with a veto in the Security
Council, so that we could get Mauritania in and get a few
votes out of the Africans.

Adlai, it always seemed, gave Francis the most difficult problems.
He was sent out on his own to handle such matters, probably because
they had known and trusted each other for such a very long time. Three
absolutely impossible things to have to try to deal with were the Arab-
Israeli conflict and Arab refugees, South African apartheid and the
financial problems of the U.N. The Pakistan-Kashmir dispute and the
Alto-Adige (or Sud Tirol, depending on the point of view) were easier.
The latter was the nearest thing to a diplomatic success that Francis
achieved.

His oral history comments on the Arab-Israeli conflict:

Right now, we're in an entirely different posture; we're being tarred, if you want to put it that way, with being the outright supporter of Israel. In those days, we tried to maintain an even balance between the Arabs and Israel. Golda Meir would spit in my eye if she saw me today, she so disliked my trying to be impartial—I don't think she really would, because she's too big a person for that, but she is the foreign potentate I came closest to having a real fight with of anybody that I ever dealt with at the U.N. However, I was in Israel the summer before last with the New York Philharmonic when she was away on vacation, and somebody in a position to know told me, to my surprise, that she held me in the highest esteem, but you certainly would never know it from the way we wrangled back and forth in the sixties. She was furious with me for not getting up and defending Israel in the Special Political Committee meetings when Ahmed Shukairy, who was then head of the Palestine Liberation Movement—actually at that time he was the U.N. delegate from Saudi Arabia. He would get up and talk for seven hours, (time out for lunch) slanging Israel up and down and backwards and forwards, vilifying them. Golda felt I ought to get up and answer him. Well, the Israelis were perfectly capable of answering for themselves; it wasn't our policy to get up and defend Israel any more than it was our policy to get up and defend the Arabs whenever the Israelis slammed them. She got really very angry that I had not gotten up and defended Israel. She said something very extreme—I can't remember exactly what it was—and I remember saying as icily as I could, that I hoped it would not be necessary for me to report to my government what she had said. At that she backed down, and we ended up on reasonably friendly terms. But there is certainly an attitude on the part of the Israelis that they can call the tune for American policy. They know their power here, and they use it; no doubt about that. . . . I would like to think that I had good relations with the Jewish groups in New York. I can remember speaking to a Jewish ladies group (B'nai B'rith) on the refugee issue where the United States was taking a stance that obviously the Jewish community didn't like at all. I started out saying that I knew they were all Americans and that they wanted to know and understand the American position on the issue as distinguished from one's own prejudices. They just took it like lambs.

He goes on about the Arab refugees, describing what was being tried in the early sixties. He characterized it with the words, "You're playing with egg shells in this area."

The Palestine refugees was a very painful experience. Both sides were absolutely intractable. Israelis, I think, behaved extremely badly, and the Arabs too, I can talk a little bit about that for the history book. The story is all in the State Department, buried somewhere, but it certainly isn't well-known.

The United States is a member of the so-called Palestine Conciliation Commission [United Nations Conciliation Commission for Palestine]. There were three members: United States, Turkey, and France. The Conciliation Commission had succeeded in getting the Israelis, after a good deal of difficulty, to unfreeze Arab bank accounts in Israel. We had quite a lot of trouble getting the Arab governments to announce to their own people that these accounts were unfrozen, that they could go and get their money. The Arabs sort of hate to admit that the Israelis will ever do anything decent. However, that project worked out pretty well. We also succeeded in getting the Israelis to release the safe deposit boxes owned by Arabs in Israel—unfreeze them.

Then we had a study made of the value, as of 1945, of Arab real estate taken over by the Israelis in what is now Israel. That was a fabulous operation—done mostly by British civil servants—valuing each parcel in terms of sales, at the time, of comparable property. It works out to some 800 million dollars worth of Arab property taken over by Israelis in 1946. The calculations were as of '45 because that was the last time there were any sales under ordinary circumstances. Well, the report really does establish one factor, the almost 800 million dollar value, yet the Israelis have never been willing to pay anything for that property.

My own view as to what ought to be done about the refugee problem is to have Israel offer to pay that billion dollars to the owners, plus interest since 1946. And I would cheerfully recommend that the United States lend the money to do it, so that you could get the money into the hands of the refugees and get them thinking about something else besides going back to Palestine.

At about the same time, the Palestine Conciliation Commission, at the instance of the State Department, retained Dr. Joseph E. Johnson, President of the Carnegie Endowment for International Peace, to explore possible solutions for the refugee problem. He spent over a year going around the Middle East, talking to the Israelis, King Hussein of Jordan, Nassar, et cetera, and also talked with the refugee leaders themselves. He presented a really viable plan for the refugee problem. His plan has never been officially published, but I think that almost everyone knows just about what it was. His suggestion was that the Israelis admit some 30,000 or so refugees a year. This would not present any danger as regards Israel's security and, at the same time, would partially comply with the U.N. General Assembly's resolution as to the return of the refugees, which provided that all refugees were entitled to return to their homes in Palestine and that those who did not wish to do so would receive compensation. His thought was that the refugees who did return would find that Israel was a very different place from the Palestine that they used to know and that the word would seep back to the refugee camps that life in Israel was not as pleasant or advantageous as would be staying in the Arab countries with a good healthy payment for Arab property in Israel.

Joe Johnson is one of the nicest and most transparently honest men of good will that I know, yet he ended up by being virtually repudiated by both the Arabs and, I think in particular, by the Israelis.

Solving the refugee problem is really, I think, the key to peace in the Middle East, but the deep emotions that persist on both sides make any solution extraordinarily difficult.

In his United Nations days, Francis especially enjoyed the challenge of working with the various Russian representatives—Zorin, Morozov, Federenko and Kuznetsov, the Deputy Foreign Minister, whom Francis always said was the nicest of them. During the Cuban missile crisis, U Thant had proposed a deal that the Russians would take out missiles, we would stop blockading Cuba, the U.N. would be allowed to inspect every so often, and we would agree not to invade. However, Castro would not let inspectors in. John J. McCloy was sent by the President to help in negotiations with Kuznetsov. Francis came back after being out with the mumps to help in the final sessions. McCloy told him that Kuznetsov had made the same hour-long speech every day and that he should be considered to have made the same rebuttal speech he had made in the very beginning. No one was getting anywhere. Finally, Francis drafted a new statement in which the two sides agreed to disagree.

Mr. Kuznetsov looked at Francis and said, "Mr. Plimpton, you remind me of a Rossian fable. A Russian peasant went to a fair. He was hongry, so he bought a loaf of white bread; still he was hongry. He bought a loaf of brown bread and still he was hongry. Finally, he bought a leetle piece of choclate cake and was no longer hongry saying, What a fool I was not to have bought the leetle piece of choclate cake in the first place. You, Mr. Plimpton, are the leetle piece of choclate cake."

The Russians loved to tell fables. One day, in connection with debate on apartheid in the Special Committee, Morozov told a story about a cat eating a fish—Francis jokingly said the fish must have been a red herring. This finally came over the translation system, and the English speaking members of the Committee smiled. Morozov was furious and pursued Francis down the corridor afterwards, saying, "I did not say that fish was a red herring—I did not say that fish was a red herring!"

The Bay of Pigs and the Cuban Missile Crisis were the most striking episodes that Adlai and Francis dealt with in those five spectacular years. Francis' oral history on the Cuban Missile Crisis also had the following interesting aside. It concerns the famous episode of the first telegram received from the Soviets upon the American demand that the freighter with the missiles be turned back. The first was conciliatory, the second belligerent.

Schlesinger gives Bobby Kennedy the credit for our answering the Soviets' first cable and ignoring the second. You may remember that there was a Friday afternoon cable from (Nikita S.) Khrushchev which was written in very "Khrushchevy," earthy style. I remember it had the very good analogy: "You, Mr. President, and I have both ends of a rope with a knot tied in the middle. The harder we pull, the tighter the knot is. If we both loosen up, maybe we can untie the knot," something like that. It was a very good sort of earthy analogy. I remember Averell Harriman said—"I'm sure that Khrushchev wrote that."

Well, in any event, when that cable came in, we, of course, got it at the same time the State Department did. The communications system is such that when something important comes from New Delhi or wherever, it hits Washington and us at the same time. And I remember shouting with glee. I said, "We've got them now!" The next morning, of course, came a long formal-cable, obviously drafted by someone else in the Russian foreign office, with all sorts of conditions and so on. I know that I said, "For Christ sakes, let's accept the first one and disregard the second." Schlesinger gives Bobby credit for that idea, but I'm sure that everybody had it; I certainly did. I remember yelling it on the telephone to somebody in Washington. I think Adlai felt the same way. This is a minor point, but I always thought that Schlesinger was giving too much credit to one person, Bobby, for an idea that certainly occurred to me, and I'm sure to Adlai and to a lot of other people.

The U.N. Congo intervention and the stalemate over Article 19 was a heartbreaking situation. Here the Soviets refused to pay their share of expenses for the peace-keeping forces in the Gaza Strip and the Sinai as well as in the Congo (the French refused also in the case of the Congo), and as they were both in arrears, should have lost their votes in the Assembly. The solution of having a no-vote Assembly was not one that Francis approved of, though he had to carry through with it. Being a lawyer, he felt they should have lost their votes and was quite furious with Ambassador Sosa Rodriguez of Venezuela, who was President of the Assembly at the time, for not being strong enough to enforce the Charter, which said firmly, "they shall have no vote."

We entertained and went to receptions avidly. Francis found them very useful for conferring informally with other Ambassadors. I learned not to stay at his coattails but would go up to people I didn't know of different nationalities and start a conversation by saying, "I'm Pauline Plimpton, U.S.A." During our first summer we had nine Sunday lunches at our house in Long Island with forty or so guests, half U.N. Ambassadors and half natives from the neighborhood. There was always a young man from the Mission to help introduce people and see to protocol. I remember only one disaster. The Mauretanian and Moroccan Ambassadors whose countries continue to have considerable differences were invited to the same party. Francis greeted the Moroccan at the door, but as they walked down to the pool, where everyone was having cocktails, the Moroccan saw the Mauretanian and refused to go a step further, but went back to find his car and go back to town. Nevertheless, the lunches were very successful and gave the representatives of other countries a chance to meet with Americans and be in an American home so that friendships would result. These occasions were much appreciated.

Being a native New Yorker, Francis was also saddled with U.N. real estate and traffic problems. He saw to it that Ambassadors were accepted when they tried to buy a cooperative apartment, not always an easy matter. He was also responsible for memberships in clubs, which meant arranging a luncheon for the prospective diplomats (of many nationalities) to meet the Board of Governors or the Membership Committee. (Diplomats in New York do not have some of the same privileges as in capital cities.) He tried unsuccessfully to persuade the Soviets that it was not wise to buy the apartment house for their headquarters which was on the same street as the Police, the Fire Department and a Jewish Synagogue. In Glen Cove, where the Soviets were in trouble over taxes on the George Pratt house they had bought, Francis persuaded them to ask the Mayor and Treasurer of Glen Cove to lunch to try to smooth matters over.

The George Pratt house was of interest to us as it was decorated in the Soviet manner with pictures of austere landscapes hung near the ceiling; there were oriental rugs and huge overstuffed armchairs, with very few small tables or decorative objects. For me, one memorable feature of the luncheon was that the caviar was served on Ritz crackers.

We went on two speaking trips in connection with the U.N., one to the Scandinavian countries and another to Africa. Francis would meet with the leaders of each country and often make speeches. He would then report back his impressions in detail to the State Department.

In Africa, we went to Senegal, the Ivory Coast, Ghana, Nigeria and the Congo, now Zaire, where Francis caught para-typhoid in Leopoldville, now Kinshasha. There is a plaque in the State Department building in Washington commemorating those who lost their lives in active duty abroad. He barely escaped having his name inscribed there!

I have chosen three speeches or writings from the many produced at this time. They give, in his own words, the essence of what he experienced, his reaction to the contacts he had with the leaders of the world and his thoughts on international affairs and the U.N.

Remarks — U.N. Day

October 28, 1975

> Being an Ambassador involved making speeches around
> the country, especially on U.N. Day or before special
> groups. It was largely an effort to inform the public.
> I remember at one American Bar Association meeting in
> Las Vegas the audience's astonishment as Francis
> revealed some of the accomplishments of the U.N. It was
> as if they had never heard of the U.N. before; they were
> quite moved. Here is one in Manhattan with Governor
> Hugh Carey and Mayor Abe Beame on the dais.

This is obviously not an occasion for unalloyed joy about the U.N., but I suggest that we do some supposing.

Suppose that in October 1945, thirty years ago in San Francisco, no Charter was agreed to and nothing was signed.

The East River between 42nd and 49th Streets would still be lined with slaughterhouses, and the air on Second Avenue would still be redolent with the smell of drying blood. To be sure, diplomatic cars would not be blocking traffic and fire hydrants, tax exempt real estate would not have burgeoned beyond belief, uncounted policemen would not be protecting that real estate and its inhabitants—*but* this City would be without an international community of some 8,000 permanent spenders and 141 spending missions; there would be no yearly influx of the world's leading statesmen and their staffs, nor 1,000,000 visitors a year to the U.N.; the City would be short U.N. connected expenditures of $200,000,000 a year and it would not be the capitol of the world.

World War II Russian troops might still be in northern Iran; Dutch soldiers and Indonesians might still be fighting in Java and Sumatra; there would be no partition of Palestine and no Israel; no Nobel Peace Prize Winner Ralph Bunche to produce Israeli-Arab armistices and no one to supervise them.

Kashmir might still be a battlefield, with no observers to keep Indians and Pakistanis apart—then, or later in Rann of Kutch when the tanks ran out of fuel; thirty nine countries would not have joined the U.S. in Korea under a U.N. flag; the 1956 war for Suez might never have been cut short or a precarious 10-year peace on the Sinai Peninsula preserved by the blue helmets; there would be no unified Zaire—only a fragmented ex-Belgian Congo riven by a separatist Katanga, a separatist Orientale and a separatist Kasai; Netherlands and Indonesia might still be quarreling over West Irian.

Heaven only knows what could have come out of the Cuban missile crisis without U Thant's formula which let Khrushchev withdraw his ICBM's without too much loss of face; Greek Cypriots and Turkish Cypriots would be at each other's throats; U.N. peacekeepers would not again be standing in Sinai and on the Golan Heights.

There would be no International Court of Justice, ready and waiting for more use; no declaration of human rights; no convention against racism; no World Bank; no I.D.A. (International Development Association); no U.N. High Commissioner for Refugees or UNRWA for Palestineans; no Nobel Peace Prize winning UNICEF with its millions for the world's children.

There would be no International Atomic Energy Agency, no agreement on the peaceful uses of outer space, no Conferences on Trade and Development or on the Environment or on the Law of the Sea or on Population, and no Food and Agricultural Organization. Abu Simbel would have been drowned by the Nile with no UNESCO; there would have been no World Meteorological Organization and, if you please, perish the thought, no International Women's Year.

Perhaps I can sum up my supposing by reminding you of the late Senator Greene of Rhode Island. On his 93rd birthday a reporter asked him: "Senator, how does it feel to be 93 years old and still alive?" He replied, "Not so bad, considering the alternative!"

What Is a Secretary General?

Francis was asked quite often to write articles for the
New York Times. This one was published in the New
York Times Magazine Section of November 27, 1966.

The tourist on his United Nations guided tour looked inquiringly at the
sweet girl guide and said "I know what a secretary is, and I know what
a general is, but what on earth is a secretary general?" The answer is
not simple.

She could quote him the Charter, but its bony phrases are but a
framework skeleton—one doesn't get much of an idea of the Presidency
of the United States from reading the Constitution.

She could point out to him, in the cavernous General Assembly
hall, the imperturbable U Thant, sitting on high above the podium on
the president's right and listening impassively to the torrent of words
surging forth below, but the sight gives no hint of the powers, rights,
obligations and responsibilities that center, not in that echoing hall, but
in a modest office on the 38th floor of the neighboring gray and green
glass slab of a Secretariat building.

Perhaps one should start with the Charter. Article 97 provides that
the Secretary General shall be appointed by the General Assembly upon
the recommendation of the Security Council. This sounds placid, but
is anything but placid, for any such recommendation by the Security
Council (requiring nine affirmative votes from the 15 members) can be
blocked by the veto of any of the permanent members—the U.S., Soviet
Union, United Kingdom, France and China. This of course means that
no candidate can possibly be appointed unless he is approved by *all* the
permanent members. Given past and present international tensions, get-

ting such unanimous approval is the equivalent of passing a major miracle.

Trygve Lie, Norwegian activist labor leader and politician, was the first to achieve the miracle. His burly and forthright support of the U.N.'s (and U.S.'s) defense of South Korea against Communist aggression earned him bitter Soviet opposition, with resulting deadlock in the Security Council when his reappointment came up in 1951. The Assembly took it upon itself, with little taint of legality, to continue him in office for three years, but the Soviet bloc refused to deal with him, and he finally resigned in 1953.

There followed Dag Hammarskjold, Swedish economist and civil servant, appointed for five years, reappointed in 1958, and serving until his tragic airplane-crash death in September, 1961, while on a Congo mission.

By this time the Soviet Union, furious at the results of Hammarskjold's conduct of the U.N.'s peacekeeping intervention in the Congo (which the votes of the Security Council, including that of the Soviet Union, had three times authorized him to conduct), insisted that there should be three Secretaries General, one Communist, one Western and one nonaligned, and that they would have to act unanimously. Quite apart from being contrary to the Charter, this proposal, for a three-horse Russian troika, was obviously designed to extend the Soviet veto to the Secretariat and thus subject the entire U.N. staff to a Communist straitjacket.

This barefaced power play got no support outside the Soviet bloc. Many, if not most, U.N. members resent the existence of the veto in the Security Council, and no non-Communist members wanted it forced on the Secretariat.

The Soviets then proposed a second-tier troika—three Under Secretaries General, one Communist, one Western and one nonaligned, all of whom would have to be consulted by the Secretary General and be in accord before any important action was taken. This imperfectly disguised veto grab also got no non-Communist support.

Finally, in 1961 after the long and ardous delay always involved in any negotiations with the Soviets (who never give up until it is overwhelmingly clear that they cannot have their way), they finally agreed to the appointment of U Thant without strings—other than his saying that he would consult his principal advisers, which of course he would do anyway.

The U.N. was lucky to have U Thant as a candidate—and is unlucky not to have him as one now. (Though he said in September that he would not seek a second term, U Thant has promised to make a final announcement of his plans by the end of this month.) As an Asian he was *persona grata* to the U.N.'s Afro-Asian majority, and his equable personality and Buddhist-Burmese equanimity and impartiality were appreciated by all. There were reservations; a leading European ambassador (guess which) tartly said, "It is out of the question—he doesn't speak French!"

So much for how a Secretary General is appointed—what does he do?

Article 97 of the Charter provides, "The Secretariat shall comprise a Secretary General and such staff as the Organization may require," and goes on to say that the Secretary General shall be "the chief administrative officer of the Organization." He administers quite a lot—in particular, some 3,900 U.N. staff members on the East River and 2,250 others spread around the world. Functionally, about a fourth of them are concerned with the political crises that crowd the headlines; the rest are involved in the economic, social and technical activities of the U.N. that get little publicity, but in the long run may well prove the organization's major contributions to a better world.

Needless to say, the Secretary General does not himself hire and fire his staff members, but he is inescapably involved in the international wrangles that accompany both processes.

Article 101 of the Charter provides: "The paramount consideration in the employment of the staff and in the determination of the conditions of service shall be the necessity of securing the highest standards of efficiency, competence and integrity. Due regard shall be paid to the importance of recruiting the staff on as wide a geographical basis as possible."

Most member governments seem to read only the second sentence of that paragraph—there is a vigorous competitive geographic scramble for the important posts and, indeed, for all the posts ("more than half the members are Afro-Asians, why shouldn't the staff be?"). Communist governments are always claiming that they are underrepresented, but they will never permit U.N. recruiting among their nationals and are slow about making recommendations to fill the vacancies constantly being caused by Communist policy against letting any comrade stay at the U.N. for more than three years (lest he be corrupted by capitalism or internationalism?)—a policy inimical to the building up of a proper international service. As to the Africans, there has been a genuine effort to get more of them in U.N. jobs, but it is difficult to find enough of them who are properly equipped—and to take those away from their own countries, where they are so much needed.

There is a myth that Americans are overrepresented in the Secretariat. It is emphatically a myth, for excluding the lower nonpolicy categories such as stenographers (where, the U.N. being where it is, it is natural to hire the natives), the U.S. is somewhat underrepresented according to the rough governing formula approved by the General Assembly, which takes into account population, budget assessment, etc. Yet Hammarskjold abjectly surrendered to the myth when he asked his experienced and able Under Secretary Andrew Cordier to resign— to the great benefit of the Columbia Graduate School of International Affairs. The U.S. Government could well supply more support for the Americans on the staff, and more initiative in recommending first-class applicants for vacancies.

As to staff firing, the Secretary General must deal, not only with the ordinary frailties of human employees, but also with the Charter's Article 100: "In the performance of their duties, the Secretary General and the staff shall not seek or receive instructions from any government or from any other authority external to the Organization. They shall refrain from any action which might reflect on their position as international officials responsible only to the Organization."

The idea of an exclusively international civil service is fairly new under the sun, and one that has been rejected in Communist quarters both overtly and covertly. It was overt when Khrushchev, after banging his shoe on his Assembly desk, said "while there are neutral countries, there are no neutral men," and when he demanded his troika of non-internationalist Secretaries General. It became overt when teddy-bearish Soviet Under Secretary Georgi Arkadyev was caught (should one say red-handed?) passing partisan notes of advice to Soviet Security Council President V. Zorin. It was and is covert when Communist staff members indulge in quiet espionage, are caught by the F.B.I. and are asked to leave the U.N. for violating Article 100 (this has not happened as often as the John Birch Society would have us believe—but it does happen).

More serious for the U.N. itself has been the seepage of confidential information from the 38th floor to the Soviet mission, a seepage so persistent that no Secretary General has found it possible, in the interest of the organization, to take any Soviet staff member completely into his confidence. And in at least one case departure had to be sought for a Soviet national whose intolerant abuse of non-Communist colleagues became intolerable.

The Charter goes on, in Article 98, to say: "The Secretary General shall act in that capacity in all meetings of the General Assembly, of the Security Council, of the Economic and Social Council, and of the Trusteeship Council . . ."

Mercifully, no one has ever insisted that the Secretary General act in *all* meetings of the Assembly and the three Councils—else each incumbent would long since have suffocated from surfeit of oratory. But the phrase does mean that the Secretary General is responsible to the Assembly and to the Councils for carrying out their decisions—often, as will be pointed out below, anything but a clear-cut task.

Article 98 further states that the Secretary General "shall perform such other functions as are entrusted to him by these organs." Narrow constructionists have claimed that this means that he can perform *only* such other function as the Assembly and the Councils specify—in other words, that he cannot do anything they do not tell him to do. But the narrow constructionists are in a small minority, not including any past or present incumbent of the office.

Article 98 concludes that "The Secretary General shall make an annual report to the General Assembly on the work of the Organization" and Article 99 provides: "The Secretary General may bring to the attention of the Security Council any matter which in his opinion may threaten the maintenance of international peace and security."

These provisions marked a conscious and definite advance in the concept of the office as compared with the League of Nations, where the Secretary General never spoke to the League's Assembly and acted in its Council as hardly anything more than recording secretary.

The League concept, drawn on the British civil service model, was of a Secretary General and Secretariat not only non-national but non-political; policy and political decisions were made and action initiated solely by the League's Assembly and Council, and not at all by its Secretary General.

The U.N. Charter, on the other hand, definitely puts the Secretary General into the political arena—more in the position of an American President. If he is to bring—or be in a position to know whether to bring—a matter to the Security Council which he thinks may threaten international peace and security, he must keep a wide-ranging investigative eye on the trouble spots of the world, and make political decisions as to what to do about them.

As far back as 1946, in the first Greek case, Trygve Lie forcefully asserted his right, even if the Security Council failed to give him authority, to make an independent investigation of a dangerous international situation. Then, Lie was supported by the Soviets; now, U Thant is criticized by the Soviets for having sent, without Security Council authorization, a special representative, Herbert de Ribbing, to Thailand and Cambodia, with those nations' consent, to mediate between them.

Trygve Lie, fresh from active political life in Norway, did not hesitate to push out the frontiers of the Secretary General's office. He produced vigorous and pointed annual reports to the General Assembly, and a cogent 10-point program for achieving international peace through the U.N.; he lobbied and memorandaed on behalf of Communist Chinese membership in the U.N., thereby irritating the U.S. Government; he strongly supported the U.N. and U.S. defense of South Korea, thereby removing the irritation of the U.S. Government and substituting that of the Soviet Government.

When, in 1953, he finally tired of being ignored by the Communists and resigned, there is little doubt that the principal U.N. members thought that, in electing an economist and career civil servant in Dag Hammarskjold, they were going to get a quiet respite from the strong activism of Trygve Lie.

They could not have been more mistaken. After a relatively calm beginning, Hammarskjold soon showed that he thought of his office—and of the U.N.—as dynamic instrumentalities capable of energetic initiative and strong action.

In 1954, Peking rejected a General Assembly resolution requesting release of the 11 U.S. airmen (of the U.N. Korean command) still held prisoner by the Communists, but Hammarskjold, acting not on the basis of the rejected resolution but on the basis of his direct authority under the Charter, went to Peking and eventually worked out the release of the airmen. He used the same "Peking Formula" in 1960, when South Africa rejected a Security Council resolution condemning apartheid, but permitted him, on the basis of his authority under the Charter, to come to South Africa in an endeavor (fruitless) to soften its racial discrimination.

In early 1956, acting on a vaguely worded Security Council resolution, he made the first of many diplomatic incursions into the Middle East, and obtained a short-lived reaffirmation of the cease-fire provisions of the Israeli-Arab armistice agreements.

Autumn of 1956 and Suez saw the real burgeoning of Secretary General initiative and executive action. Hammarskjold was the draftsman of the six principles adopted by the Security Council for the settlement of the conflict over Nasser's seizure of the Canal; when the

Israelis, British and French invaded Egypt and the Security Council, blocked by British and French vetoes, referred the crisis to the General Assembly, the Assembly requested Hammarskjold to set up a plan for an emergency U.N. force to secure and supervise the cessation of hostilities.

It was Hammarskjold himself, then, who devised the plan for the U.N. force on the Gaza Strip which still keeps Israelis and Egyptians from each other's throats, and it was he to whom the General Assembly delegated authority to carry the plan out. Again, it was Hammarskjold whom the Assembly authorized to arrange for the clearing of the Canal.

One of the most tragic concurrences in history was the Israeli-British-French Suez invasion and the revolt for freedom in Hungary. Had it not been for that invasion, the world's attention would have been concentrated solely on the bloody brutality of Soviet tanks and not distracted by Mediterranean gunfire, and U.N. action might have been effective; as it was, all the Assembly could do was to call on Hammarskjold to do what he could do—which was all too little.

In 1958, Hammarskjold went ahead and enlarged the U.N. observation group in Lebanon in the face of a Soviet veto of the Security Council resolution authorizing the enlargement (the veto came because the resolution did not include a demand for the immediate withdrawal of U.S. troops). Also, he had no hesitation in 1960 in responding to an invitation by the Laotian Government to investigate its troubles at firsthand, despite the lack of any Council or Assembly authority and despite considerable irritation on the part of the U.S. Government.

It was in the Congo, however, that the role of the Secretary General reached its political apogee. When, after the Congo became independent in June, 1960, the Congolese Army revolted and chaos followed, the Congolese Government called on the U.N. for military assistance (the U.S. having wisely refused), and the Security Council authorized the Secretary General "to take the necessary steps, in consultation with the Government of the Republic of the Congo, to provide the Government with such military assistance as may be necessary until, through the efforts of the Congolese Government with the technical assistance of the United Nations, the national security forces may be able, in the opinion of the Government, to meet fully their tasks . . ."

This vague mandate, voted for by the Soviet Union, provided virtually the only guideline for the Secretary General's conduct of four years of U.N. peacekeeping operations in that war-torn country.

For a while the U.N. consensus which had produced the unanimous

Security Council resolution continued; then, after the expulsion from the Congolese Government of Soviet-favorite Lumumba and his arrest and murder, Soviet support for the operation turned into bitter opposition. Cold-war clouds darkened the Congolese horizon; mineral-rich Katanga declared its independence; other provinces revolted; mercenaries abounded; a rival government proclaimed itself in Stanleyville; conflicting ambitions of other African countries contributed to the chaos; the Central Government was in disarray.

What was the Secretary General, in charge of U.N. forces finally amounting to more than 20,000 men, to do in the face of these developments? Nothing in the resolutions which formed his mandate provided any answer; the Security Council and the General Assembly were in angry and confused stalemate.

Hammarskjold, that most articulate of Secretary Generals, put the dilemma accurately. Should the Secretary General, to avoid offending one or another group of members, take the easy way out and refuse to implement a mandate on the ground that implementation would be opposed to some members' positions? Should he, for example, have abandoned the Congolese operation because almost any decision he made would have been contrary to some members' strongly held views?

His answer was that, even in the absence of any formal decision by the Security Council or the Assembly, the Secretary General had a duty to go ahead in the light of his exclusively international obligations under the Charter and in the light of the principles and purpose set forth in the Charter. He should be guided by U.N. decisions, but in the absence of such guidance should act to fill a vacuum. The U.N. is a whole greater than the sum of its parts, and the Seretary General is uniquely equipped to function as a spokesman for that whole.

So ahead Hammarskjold went, making Congo decisions as he thought an impartial internationalist should make them, regardless of unparalleled Soviet vituperation (Zorin accused him of having Lumumba's blood on his hands), bitter criticism from certain British governmental and commercial circles, the anguish of Belgian mining interests and the loud displeasure of the U.S. Katanga lobby, and causing General de Gaulle to call the U.N. "that thing."

All the while, as his posthumous diary, "Markings", discloses, he was in an inner mystical turmoil of self-analysis almost messianic in its emotional intensity—but no sign of it showed in the icy blue-eyed compousture with which he answered calumny with calm and reasoned (but somewhat complicated and hard-to-understand) dialectic. In the end he was a tragic sacrifice to his dedication to the Congo task.

When U Thant was finally chosen Secretary General, the membership clearly expected a much less controversial conduct of the office from the mild-mannered Burmese than they had had from his incisive predecessor.

Yet it was U Thant, in the face of acrid opposition from many British, French, Belgian and American quarters, who finally ordered the U.N. Congo troops to use force against Moise Tshombe and his mercenaries and end Katangan obstructionism. It was he who, without waiting for Security Council or General Assembly authority, arranged to send U.N. troops to supervise the U.N.'s interim administration of West New Guinea, and U.N. observers to watch over the tumult that followed the overthrow of the Yemen royal Government and the substitution of a somewhat shaky (now United Arab Republic-dominated) republic.

Also, in the Cuban missile crisis, it was his appeal to Chairman Khrushchev and President Kennedy which, as President Kennedy later said, greatly facilitated the eventual solution; it was much easier for Khrushchev to yield, as on the face of things he did, to an appeal from the Secretary General than, as in fact he did, to the power of the United States.

Nor has U Thant been reticent in voicing, especially in press conferences, his untrammeled ideas on international matters. Thus, at the height of the Katanga crisis, he blithely referred to the Katangan authorities as "a bunch of clowns," only to have "clown" Tshombe become Prime Minister of the Congo not long after. In May, 1964, he said, with respect to Senator Goldwater's suggestion that atomic bombs be used in South Vietnam, that anybody who proposes the use of atomic weapons for destructive purposes is out of his mind.

Just after Khrushchev's dismissal, U Thant fluttered Kremlin dovecotes by saying that it would be desirable to have Khrushchev make a public statement on the circumstances leading to his exit. In February, 1965, U Thant not only fluttered but rocked White House dovecotes by saying that he was sure the American people, if only they knew the true facts and the background of developments in South Vietnam, would agree that further bloodshed was unnecessary, adding that in times of war the first casualty is truth (an anguished "clarification," put out the next day on his behalf by the 38th floor, was only partly soothing).

U Thant's refreshing frankness in answering press-conference questions (no matter how provocatively needling) is evidence of his transparent and guileless honesty, but his well-wishers (he has no ill-wishers), would heave a sigh of relief if he never talked to a newspaperman again in his life.

On the other hand, U Thant has been conspicuously careful not to take a position on cold-war issues between the so-called Great Powers (why is it that the word "power" is so often used in an organization supposedly devoted to the non-use of power?). Thus, in the financial crisis caused by Communist and French refusal to pay for their share of the expense of peacekeeping operations they did not like, and the consequent dispute as to whether under Article 19 of the Charter they were deprived of their vote in the Assembly, U Thant, despite the fact that the financial future of his organization was at stake, never threw the weight of his office behind the Charter and its interpretation by the International Court of Justice and by the overwhelming vote of the Assembly; instead he preserved a posture of nonalignment characterized by many as gelatinous. An Eastern European ambassador, on being asked recently whether the Communists would again press for a troika, unkindly remarked, having in mind U Thant's noteworthy unwillingness to take any position on a cold-war issue, "Why should we; we have a troika right now."'

However, one must be realistic in measuring the practical possibilities that are open to a Secretary General of the United Nations, taking into account the political limitations that hem him in. The experience of Trygve Lie and Dag Hammarskjold shows that strong stands taken between the Great Powers tend to wrack and wreck the incumbent (with the possibility of doing the same to the U.N. itself), and some would argue that the cause of compromise and peace is better served, given the present rudimentary and somewhat fragile state of international organization, by a Secretary General who sidesteps instead of stepping up.

U Thant's appointment last August of a special representative to Cambodia and Thailand, with their consent, to help eliminate the tension between them, has already been mentioned. When he reported the appointment to the Security Council, the Soviet representative promptly wrote the President of the Security Council that only the Security Council could decide such matters. The Argentine representative stoutly replied that the Secretary General's action was fully justified and within his competence, and the Uruguayan representative promptly concurred.

There the matter rests, but there is no doubt as to what U Thant meant when, in his press conference of Sept. 19, he said that he had found it increasingly difficult to function in the manner in which he wishes to function, and that he did not subscribe to the view that he should be just a chief administrative officer or, in other words, a glorified clerk. Beside administrative functions, he said, the Secretary General must take necessary initiatives in the political and diplomatic fields, and such initiatives are an essential part of his functions. The attempted straitjacketing of the office by the Communists and French is undoubtedly one of the principal reasons for U Thant's statement that he would not offer himself for another term.

It is clear that there are sharply varying ideas as to what the powers and functions of the Secretary General are and should be.

The Soviet position has always been, and still is, that the Secretary General is a purely administrative officer whose only function is to implement prior decisions by the Security Council and the General Assembly. In particular, he must take no step having to do with the maintenance of international peace and security without the prior specific authorization of the Security Council. This, of course, ties in with Soviet insistence that the Security Council has the sole and only right to authorize, conduct and determine the expenses of anything having to do with the maintenance of peace, and that the General Assembly has no such right.

The French view seems to be much the same, although the French, who bitterly criticized as unlawful intervention any involvement by the U.N. or the Secretary General in the Algerian conflict or in the Congo, applauded U.N. and Secretary General involvement in the Dominican Republic situation—an involvement regarded by the U.S. and Latin Americans as unnecessary and prejudicial to what turned out to be the beneficial result of the action by the U.S. and the Organization of American States.

The U.S Government has generally supported the concept of a strong Secretary General, capable of taking decisive and independent action, especially when inaction or stalemate of the Security Council or General Assembly has created a vacuum. U.S. enthusiasm has cooled, however, when the action turned out to be troublesome for U.S. interests—witness Washington impatience not only with U Thant's observers in the Dominican Republic but with his one-sided (to U.S. ears) recommendations for peace in Vietnam.

The simple truth is that any government's attitude toward the office of Secretary General and its powers will inevitably vary with what the incumbent does and how it affects what the government considers to be its interest. But surely it is to the interest of all governments to have the office filled by an incumbent of the integrity, impartiality and independence of U Thant, and to have him, after he contemplates the dangerous and chaotic conflict sure to be involved in the attempt to agree on a successor, * consent to have the office continue to be filled by himself.

---

*Francis was intending to add to this article by commenting on the next two incumbents, Kurt Waldheim of Austria and Javier Pérez de Cuéllar of Peru.

They Sent You Our Best

At the sad moment of Adlai Stevenson's death in London in 1965, Francis became Acting U.S. Ambassador to the United Nations. He was responsible and made all the arrangements for the Memorial Service for Adlai in New York which was held in the Assembly Hall of the United Nations. Francis persuaded Archibald MacLeish to speak, which he did most eloquently, as did Dean Rusk, then Secretary of State. Francis almost broke down as he presided. The Chief of Protocol leaned towards him after the speeches, worried as to how the occasion was to end. Francis had decided to finished with the poignant words that come at the end of this essay. For a book of reminiscences of friends of Adlai Stevenson, called "As We Knew Adlai", Francis contributed his recollections. His title is taken from the words of Dean Rusk at the Memorial Service: "Three Presidents of the United States sent Adlai Stevenson to the United Nations.
They sent you our best.''

The United Nations Charter contemplates that each member state shall have a "permanent representative" at the headquarters district.

Adlai Stevenson filled that always exacting, often exasperating, sometimes exciting, inevitably exhausting and occasionally exhilarating post on behalf of the United States, with the rank of Ambassador Extraordinary and Plenipotentiary, from January 23, 1961, until his sudden death on the streets of London on July 14, 1965.

He was an old hand at the U.N. He was at San Francisco at its birth as an Assistant to Secretary of State Stettinius and as an advisor to the U.S. delegation, and he was chief of the U.S. delegation to the U.N. Preparatory Commission in London in 1946, and a member of the U.S. delegation to the First and Second U.N. General Assemblies in 1946 and 1947.

So, when Adlai Stevenson came back to the U.N. in January, 1961, it was a homecoming. But it was more than that; there was in him no sense of a relaxing return to a familiar resting place, rather the stimulus of a known but challenging platform as a launching base for the hopes of the future.

His first press conference on January 27, 1961, was unforgettable. Committee Room 4 in the U.N. basement is, oddly, the biggest: low-ceilinged but wide and broad, crammed, that afternoon, with the U.N. press corps—the largest in the world—Europeans, Asians, Communists, Africans, stringers, hangers-on, delegates. There was an electric quality of anticipation, of curiosity, of friendliness.

In he came with that quick, preoccupied walk, the slightly baggy, gray tweed coat, the almost shy side glances, along behind the long blond writing desk and blond fixed chairs, until he came toward the center chair and the microphones and stood silent, erect, as the standing crowd exploded in applause. And then that sudden, delighted smile that transformed thoughtfulness into pleased awareness, into glowing acceptance of the warmth of welcome.

First, an off-the-cuff, lighthearted reference to his own newspaper past, and then his prepared statement, eloquent in its evocation of the U.N.'s past and of what might and should be its future, and of the United States' determination to strengthen and expand its influence and authority.

"Eloquent" never seems quite the right word for Stevenson—it sounds too much like elocution. It is true that his words had a soaring quality; but it was not the words themselves that lifted us up, it was the soaring mind and spirit behind those words.

Being an ambassador to—or, rather, at—the U.N. is like no other post in the diplomatic—or any other—world. An ordinary ambassador deals with only one government; at the U.N. one is dealing with the representatives and delegates of 116 (with more to come), plus a Secretary General and the Secretariat. At the usual post the other ambassadors are colleagues in the merely social sense; at the U.N. they represent votes, and the day has long since passed when the United

States did not need votes and need to work hard to get them.

So a U.S. Ambassador at the U.N. needs the flexibility to negotiate successfully with Latin Americans, Communists, Arabs, Israelis, Pakistanis, Indians, Africans (French- or English-speaking)—the whole gamut of the diverse peoples of our turbulent world. He needs broad and deep background knowledge of these countries and problems; he should know their leaders and like them. He should be able to understand conflicting and contradictory positions and devise acceptable compromises, without sacrificing principle.

As Secretary of State Dean Rusk said at the U.N. memorial ceremony for Adlai Stevenson on July 19, 1965, the United Nations "calls out for the best that can be produced by the societies of man. Three Presidents of the United States sent Adlai Stevenson to the United Nations. They sent you our best."

He was our best. It was not only that he had been an adviser at San Francisco and an experienced Assembly delegate in the past; it was that he came to the world organization as a true man of the world—not in terms of sophistication (although he was sophisticated in the best sense of the word) but in terms of knowledge of the whole world and understanding of the whole world.

If the name of an obscure airport in the Congo came up in debate, he had been there; the prime minister of the newly admitted member state he had stayed with; his first trip to the Soviet Union was in 1926; there could not be more than six or so of the 116 U.N. members whose capitals he had not visited and with whose leaders he had not talked.

He was a master of words, and words matter at the U.N. Its councils, assemblies and committees act by resolutions, and resolutions are words, words fought over, dissected, shaded, sharpened, blunted, fused or defused. Which shall it be: "Recalling," "mindful of" or "reaffirming"? "Requests," "urges," "calls upon" or "demands"? "Regrets," "deplores," "condemns" or "denounces"? Many times his would be the phrase that would reconcile the apparently irreconcilable.

But, above all, he came to the U.N. equipped with moderation and reason. These are not prevalent qualities in that glass house where people do throw stones, where emotion too often does run rampant and where vituperation too often does supplant debate. His low, calm, measured voice was all the more effective in contrast to the invective which he so often had to listen and reply to.

One cannot be what is in effect an ambassador to 116 governments without knowing their representatives and delegates—whence that activity known in the State Department budget as "representation"—i.e., entertainment.

Whatever a diplomatic reception—i.e., cocktail party—may be like in Washington or in other capitals, the U.N. variety is work. You are after votes, after information; you want someone to sponsor a resolution; you want someone else to agree to an amendment; and everyone else wants something from you. The result is a constant series of minor (or major) negotiations and fencing matches, with almost always a grist of meaningful news or surmise for the nightly information telegrams to the Department in Washington (and for the repeats to interested capitals).

The Governor did not enjoy these functions—particularly when there were four or five an evening (he defined U.N. social life as "protocol, alcohol and Geritol"). He preferred, and rightly, to talk and listen in quiet and not in an alcoholic din. The result was that his staff sometimes had to prod him, virtually with a cattle goad, to get him to go to a particular reception. Once at it, he would display an unerring eye for some side exit he could slip quietly out of without being seen by the receiving line—indeed, his knowledge of New York hotel ballroom kitchen exits was extensive and notorious.

His own entertainments were something else again. The top floor (twelfth) of the United States Mission building, across U.N. Plaza (First Avenue) from the U.N., is virtually all one glass-enclosed room, with a curious, slightly concave ceiling. There are striking night views to the west and north of the brilliantly lit wall of skyscrapers and to the east of the black river and Long Island City, beyond the top of the General Assembly building and the gleaming slab of the Secretariat.

There he produced some memorable evenings: his own Second City (i.e., Chicago) satirists, some of whose savage barbs would have sent them to Siberia if they had been playing in Moscow and had dealt with Soviet policy as they did on the twelfth floor with American; American folk singers redolent of the American past—and they, too, bluntly frank about some of the American present; and good dance music that kept the last Latin Americans dancing until the small-houred lights figuratively winked good night.

He liked better the quieter entertaining at the U.S. Embassy—for so reads the shield over Apartment 42-A, forty-two floors up at the Waldorf Astoria Towers at Park Avenue and Fiftieth Street. It is one of the most attractive places to live in New York: a lovely white Louis XV living room with spectacular views of the East River and the Grand Central towers (alas, the latter are blotting out the faraway Wall Street pinnacles), a gracious smaller living room and a charming dining room, all beautifully furnished (credit the Henry Cabot Lodges) and adorned with paintings he borrowed from museums and friends—Sargent, Thomas Hart Benton, Childe Hassam, Corot, Monet, Goya—and his own things—original Lincoln letters, a Valentine from and drawn by Jacqueline Kennedy, the medaled freedom of the City of New York, books galore.

Here he entertained steady kaleidoscopic streams of U.N. people and friends—breakfast with a foreign minister (an old friend), lunch for Latin Americans in honor of a new ambassador (gracefully amusing and warm words of welcome), working drinks with the top British, dinner for Middle Eastern head of state, music by a gifted young American pianist and supper—not, of course, a daily schedule, but not far from it.

In a sense a U.S. Ambassador to the U.N. is a U.N. Ambassador to the U.S. Stevenson certainly was. Of the literally thousands of invitations to speak that poured in on him from all around the country, he accepted almost more than he should have—out of conviction that it was part of his mission to talk sense to the American people (shades of 1952) about the U.N. and the position of the United States in the U.N. and in the world. And talk sense he did, at conventions and conferences and dinners from Boston to New Orleans to Chicago to Dallas (where a Birch lady smote him with an anti-U.N. sign) to San Francisco.

How he worried and worked over those speeches. Usually he would outline some ideas to someone on the staff, who would come up with a draft; then he would start redrafting (often completely), revising, polishing until the last hectic deadline, never satisfied, but satisfying the listeners, for he *did* talk sense, uncommon common sense, about the U.N., the U.S. and the world.

Speeches at the U.N. itself in a way went through the same process but in a way were something else again. USUN (namely, U.S. Mission to the U.N.) is on the other end of several leased telephone lines to the State Department—a situation which has its advantages and disadvantages. Actually, they are in theory all advantages, since the closer any embassy is to its principal the better, but it depends on the point of view.

There is probably not a single U.S. mission (a word which embraces embassies, legations, etc.) anywhere that is not profoundly convinced that it knows much more about what U.S. policy in its area should be than does the State Department. USUN is not immune to this conviction as to its area (the whole world, if you please), and it is certainly true that USUN is in a unique close-up position, as observer and as participant, to analyze the international problems and crises that crowd the U.N.'s agenda and to evaluate the shifting currents of world opinion that swirl through the U.N.'s halls.

But the fact (and it is a fact) remains that U.S. policy at the U.N. is—and should be—finally determined in the State Department. Only there can reports from all the world's capitals (not only the sounding board of the U.N.) be correlated, and only there can the views and interests of Congress and the country at large and of other governmental departments and agencies be taken fully into account in the formulation of final foreign policy decisions.

What actually happens over those leased telephone lines is a constant USUN-State Department dialogue—indeed negotiation—as to exactly what instructions USUN should get (a sometimes heard USUN saying is that it's easier to deal with the Soviets than with the department).

Stevenson was an active and vigorous participant in those dialogues, and usually carried the day—and it must not be forgotten that he was a member of the Cabinet (and the New York-Washington airline shuttle's most constant patron)* and thus intimately involved in the working out of fundamental American foreign policy.

All of this means that Stevenson's speeches in the U.N. (locally called statements or interventions) were conglomerates of State Department drafts, USUN and AES objections (sometimes substantive and always stylistic) and redrafts, occasional White House arbitrations of those objections, and eventual hard-fought cease-fires and compromises.

No matter how confused the exact parentage of Stevenson's U.N. speeches may have been, they invariably bore his stamp of clarity and vividness (often added in the last postdepartment clearance minute), and they most certainly reached what was for the U.N. unprecedented heights of reasoned intelligence—just as did his 1952 and 1956 presidential campaign speeches for the United States.

Speeches do not make the U.N. go around; negotiations do, and they are endless. One remembers the interminable Stevensonian palavers after Dag Hammarskjold's tragic death, fighting off repeated Soviet

---

*From Francis' oral history: "This U.N. operation is a very demanding one, and the idea that you can spend one or two days a week in Washington and do the job up here is just out of the question. You can't do it. Adlai had an office down there, a little cubbyhole in the assistant secretary's office. He would try to get down there to Cabinet meetings and so on—but it was almost hopeless."

attempts to hamstring the U.N. with a three-headed troika, and finally working out the election of an unfettered U Thant; constant conferences with the Secretary General and Secretariat officials and with other delegations as to U.N. peace-keeping efforts in the Congo, along Israeli-Arab borders, in West Irian, Kashmir, Yemen and Cyprus; repeated (and repetitive) negotiations with the Soviets on virtually all the U.N.'s thorny problems and crises.

Soviet negotiating technique is almost invariable: to restate at each meeting in wearisome detail each and every Soviet argument on the point in issue, no matter how many times previously made and previously answered or refuted. It is as though the negotiator were afraid (maybe he is) that a verbatim record of the session might not show, on Kremlin examination, proper 100 percent zeal for each and every Communist contention. (When negotiating in the Soviet Mission one was always tempted to poke the sofa to try to locate the machine that *was* making the verbatim record.)

Stevenson's patience during these ordeals was proverbial. He would listen as attentively as though he had never heard the arguments before, and would then calmly go ahead with his quiet attempts to find solutions rather than debating triumphs. He always sought success, not victory.

He showed much the same patience in enduring the floods of public oratory that engulf U.N. councils, assemblies and committees (one sometimes forgets that our Senators and Congressmen also are known to talk interminably for home consumption).

Sometimes his patience wore thin. After listening in the Security Council to hours of wild African outbursts misrepresenting and denouncing the Stanleyville rescue operations (when American planes dropped Belgian paratroopers to save hundreds of hostages—European and other—held ready for murder by rebel savages), he said:

> I have served in the United Nations from the day of its inception off and on for seventeen years. But never before have I heard such irrational, irresponsible, insulting and repugnant language in these chambers—and language used, if you please, contemptuously to impugn and slander a gallant and successful effort to save human lives of many nationalities and colors.

The Cuba episodes, Bay of Pigs and missiles, deserve separate mention by themselves.

In April, 1961, a young CIA representative came into the then USUN
gloomy offices at 2 Park Avenue and guardedly indicated to Stevenson
and top USUN personnel that something was likely to happen on the
shores of the erstwhile republic. The financing was to be by Cuban
émigrés; no U.S. facilities were to be involved (perhaps an abandoned
U.S. Army post for preliminary training, which, at USUN urging, would
again be abandoned); the impression of one listener, at least, was that
there would be a succession of clandestine night landings until a real
Oriente force was built up—no hint of any overt frontal assault.

When what did happen happened, USUN was as surprised as anyone
else. Stevenson accepted as true the CIA story of defecting Castro pilots
bombing Castro airfields, and the CIA photography of the supposed
Castro planes that had done it—which in good faith he showed the
U.N. General Assembly's First Committee. The disclosure that these
were fakes caused him wounds over which the scar tissue never completely healed.

Easier to deal with was the claim that in some unexplained way
Stevenson, who knew nothing about the true nature of the Bay of Pigs
exercise, had some part in President Kennedy's decision not to permit
U.S. direct air power to be involved. Suffice it to quote the November
1, 1961, telegram of apology to Stevenson from General Van Fleet
(emphatically not an admirer of the Governor), who had said in a speech
that U.S. air cover for the Cuban invasion had been called off at Stevenson's insistence:

> My information from several sources regarding Cuba
> was evidently erroneous in view of your telegram, which I
> am glad to have. I stand corrected and am sorry for press
> statement which was, in fact, not accurate and completely
> out of context.

Stevenson was involved in the Cuban missile crisis almost from the
start, in Washington first and then at the U.N. Leaving aside the question
of exactly where he stood as between administration hawks and doves
(he was very near the JFK middle), it is clear that his advice was of
crucial importance in the wise decision to take the matter to the U.N.
Security Council—wise because it made it much easier for Khrushchev
to accept (i.e., back down before) a U.N. appeal than would have been
the case if only the United States had been involved.

The Security Council meeting of October 25, 1962, was unforgettable. Stevenson opened with a sober and restrained defense of the declaration by the United States of its naval and air quarantine (read "blockade") against the introduction into Cuba of nuclear weapons and equipment, and pointed out that the united action of the Western Hemisphere nations was in necessary defense against the threat of offensive nuclear weapons clandestinely installed in Cuba by the Soviet Union.

The Cuban representative followed, saying that Stevenson had not produced any serious evidence that Cuba constituted a nuclear threat to the Western Hemisphere.

Then came Zorin, the Soviet President (for the month) of the Security council. A heavy, tough Communist hatchet man, with a face like a battle-ax, he was the engineer of the armed Soviet coup that overthrew the democratic government of Czechoslovakia and turned that unhappy country into one of the most abject of the Soviet satellites.

In his high Russian voice, savage with scornful sarcasm, Zorin attacked the United States as an aggressive bandit threatening international peace by an illegal blockade, and tauntingly claimed that the United States had no evidence of any Soviet nuclear build-up in Cuba except fake evidence produced by the CIA.

STEVENSON (who had been busily scribbling during the translations of Zorin's diatribe—in the Security Council every speech is consecutively translated into English and French even though it has already been simultaneously translated in the earphones): I want to say to you, Mr. Zorin, that I do not have your talent for obfuscation, for distortion, for confusing language and for double-talk—and I must confess to you that I am glad I do not . . .

ZORIN: I am not in an American court of law, and therefore do not wish to answer a question put to me in the manner of a prosecuting counsel. You will receive the answer in due course in my capacity as representative of the Soviet Union.

STEVENSON: You are in the courtroom of world opinion right now, and you can answer "yes" or "no.". . . I am prepared to wait for my answer until Hell freezes over, if that is your decision. I am also prepared to present the evidence in this room.

In point of fact USUN had received, two days before, the U-2 photographs showing the missile installations, but had been instructed not to show them—although they had just been inadvertently published in London. (One reason given was that they had to be kept for Press Secretary Salinger's Sunday night TV broadcast!) Also, Stevenson was all against showing them, since he had never forgotten his traumatic experience in 1961 of showing in the U.N. fake CIA photographs of defecting Castro bombers that were supposed to have bombed Cuban airfields before the Bay of Pigs—and knew that the Russians had never forgotten it.

But Zorin's taunts and USUN insistence had brought Stevenson around, and an urgent USUN telephone call to Secretary Rusk at the White House got permission to use the photographs—with the result that Stevenson, in that never-to-be-forgotten scene, spread before the Security Council, and the world, the convincing visual proof of the Soviet clandestine nuclear threat to the United States and to the Western Hemisphere.*

It is an interesting footnote, and sidelight on the impression Stevenson made on others at the U.N., that on the day after Stevenson's death, Zorin, who had long since left the U.N., had been a Deputy Soviet Foreign Minister and was then Soviet Ambassador to France, made a personal call on U.S. Ambassador Bohlen in Paris to express his personal sympathy at Stevenson's death.

As Ambassador Sosa-Rodriguez, the Venezuelan President of the U.N.'s Eighteenth General Assembly, said at the memorial ceremony for Stevenson held in the Assembly Hall on July 19, 1965:

> Adlai Stevenson, like all public men, has been known
> to have devoted admirers and formidable adversaries, but
> he has never been known to have enemies. And it is because
> the goodness and sincerity that flowed from his personality
> could not allow for feelings of enmity to be forged against
> him.

The ceremony itself was memorable. The great hall and the balconies

---

*Francis had the easel and the photographs concealed in a room outside the Security Council and had rewritten the text supplied by the Navy describing the pictures the night before to make it more intelligible. He made the call to Secretary Rusk as the meeting was going on and got permission to show them.

and the corridors were filled with the U.N. and with the great of New York. A minute of complete and poignant silence; tributes of moving sincerity by U Thant and Ambassador Sosa-Rodriguez; perceptive and deeply felt words from poet and friend Archibald MacLeish:

> What we have lost, as he said of his friend, Mrs. Roo-
> sevelt, is not his life. He lived that out, if not to the full,
> at least more fully than almost any other man. What we
> have lost is himself. And who can name the warmth and
> richness of it?

And from Secretary of State Rusk, his colleague, with moving affection:

> . . . it has been said, over and over again, that Adlai
> Stevenson was a universal man. And so he was. But not
> merely because he was informed, well traveled, urbane,
> sophisticated, eloquent and gifted; he was all of these. But
> his universality did not rest upon his being a prince among
> plain men, but upon his being a plain man even among
> princes. His was the simplicity of fundamental human val-
> ues—with what is permanent in the midst of change: the
> love of peace, the instinct of tolerance; the feeling of com-
> passion; the devotion to human rights; the urge to act for
> human welfare.

And then the final words of the presider:

> This ceremony has ended. The memory and influence
> of Adlai Stevenson have not ended.

● ● ●

Adlai's death was a traumatic experience for Francis. President Lyndon Johnson accepted his conventional resignation from the U.N. as well as those of most of the rest of the U.S. Mission except for Charles Yost, a career ambassador, a close friend of Francis. The Pres-ident appointed Justice of the Supreme Court Arthur Goldberg in Adlai's place. Charles Yost replaced Francis and subsequently became the U.S. Ambassador to the U.N.

Francis rejoined his Law Firm. Fortunately, the honors and invitations that continued to come to him from the diplomatic world helped to keep him from regretting leaving a field which he had found so engaging and stimulating. Nominated by the State Department and elected by the General Assembly to represent the United States in 1966, he was asked to serve on the Administrative Tribunal of the United Nations. This Tribunal is an international court which decides disputes brought against the management from staff members of the Secretariat and certain other organizations.

The Tribunal has seven members. The President was a brilliant French woman, Mme. Suzanne Bastid, a professor of International Law at the Sorbonne. She was succeeded as President by an Indian from Madras, who afterwards became Minister of Finance and then of Defence, Mr. R. Venkataraman. A succession of Britishers including Lord Crook and Sir Roger Stevens, former Ambassador to Iran and Sweden, a Zairian who spoke little English and often didn't arrive for the meetings, a Uruguayan who once had to flee over a change of government, a Cypriote and a Hungarian, Dr. Endre Ustor, who later became President of the Tribunal.

Most impressive, according to Francis, was Mme. Bastid. She held everyone up to the highest, most meticulous standards. The Tribunal met for three weeks in the spring in Geneva, where fruit trees and tulips were at their height, and in the fall in New York. Every opinion had to be written in both English and French and then read aloud.

Working closely with Mme. Bastid as President, Francis served as First Vice President from 1971. In 1972, she asked him to be one of six (all the rest were Frenchmen) to speak on her behalf at the ceremonies when she became a member of L'Academie des Sciences Morales et Politique in Paris, the first woman to receive this honor. It had been customary in the past to present new members with a sword. Francis said in his somewhat fractured French that the custom was not really necessary in the case of Mme. Bastid as she already had a sword—her brilliant mind. Actually, they did present her with a sword—in the dimensions of a lapel pin!

Francis served fourteen years, resigning in 1980 over the protests of his colleagues. They honored him with a plaque saying that he had provided them, coming as they did from different parts of the world, with a rather special window on American life at its best.

In tennis clothes at Borderland,
North Easton, Massachusetts, 1932.

The family in 1937 at the new house in West Hills, Huntington, Long
Island. The children, from left to right: F.T.P.P. Jr., Sarah, Oakes and
George.

Advising Stevenson about to speak for the United States during a debate in the General Assembly on a Soviet item on Chinese representation, October 22, 1962. (United Nations)

Sitting behind Adlai Stevenson in the Security Council during the showing of the U-2 photographs of the Soviet missile installations in Cuba, October 25, 1962. (United Nations)

Presiding over the Memorial Ceremony for Adlai Stevenson, July 19, 1965. (United Nations)

Speaking at the United Nations with Arthur Goldberg at his right. (Max Machol—United Nations)

*In Minneapolis for the opening
of the Tyrone Guthrie theater.*

*With the bullhorn at the steps of the Capitol during the Lawyers' Peace
March on Washington protesting the invasion of Cambodia, May 20,
1970.*

PART THREE

The Association
of the Bar
of the City
of New York

The Association of the Bar of the City of New York

Back in his law firm and again in the private sector, Francis was elected President of the Association of the Bar of the City of New York for 1968–1970. This meant that for two years the Firm lent him to the Bar for seventy-five percent of his time. There he had the good fortune to be president for the One Hundredth Anniversary.

He was a liberal, open-minded President, especially influencing the opinions of the younger lawyers towards the stuffiness of the Bar and the Establishment; he encouraged them to form a junior association but staying within the organization. He was given credit for dramatic changes. Under the influence of his presidency, the City Bar endorsed the ERA and abortion on demand, advocated the extension of legal services and took a liberal position on lawyer advertising. Two of his most important actions were taking the responsibility for the use of the Great Hall of the Association for a meeting opposing the appointment of Judge George Harrold Carswell to the Supreme Court, and secondly, his leadership of the trip of New York lawyers to Washington to protest the invasion of Cambodia. Nothing like this had ever happened in the history of the Association. He acquired a reputation of fairness and balanced thinking that resulted in my being asked more times than I can count, "What does Francis think?"

The following speeches, made in his role as President and ex-President, tell us what he did think about the important issues of the time, strangely relevant for today.

Freedom House Dinner

October 14, 1969

Freedom House is a Memorial Building to Wendell
Willkie, started during World War II. The dinner
was in honor of Chief Justice Earl Warren.

Charles Warren's "The Supreme Court in United States History" starts
out with these words:

> "The history of the United States has been written not
> merely in the halls of Congress, in the Executive offices
> and on the battle fields, but to a great extent in the chambers
> of the Supreme Court of the United States. In the largest
> proportion of cases submitted to its judgment every decision
> becomes a page of history."

What a full chapter of history, Mr. Chief Justice, the Court has
written under your leadership!

Some pages some people wonder about.

One is uneasy that the pages on obscenity apparently won't let us
even file a complaint against Portnoy*, and one wishes that somewhere
there had been a page holding that some taxpayer was right.

Some are as puzzled as are the pages, as to what the proper distance
is between state and church, and some are not sure that some of the
pages are completely reasonable as to what are unreasonable searches
and seizures.

Conflicting concerns will always conflict, and it is a matter of judg-

---

**Portnoy's Complaint* by Philip Roth was a notoriously libidinous novel.

ment as to which concern should be judged more important at any given time, but given the particular time in which we are now living, there are some who are concerned that the Court's concern for the accused as against society may not have been slightly overjudged as compared with the Court's concern for society as against crime.

But how magnificent the chapter really is! How bold and forthright the writing, how unafraid the march forward of the words, how firm, Mr. Chief Justice, the convictions of your courage! How deeply felt the urge to make equal the rights of all those whom our Declaration of Independence declared to have been created free and equal!

How misleading, in a way, is the text of our tonight's award—it speaks of the long struggle for the rights of man as though those rights already existed somewhere, and as though all one had to do was to break through barbed wire fortifications to find them ready made and liberate them.

The human rights that the Warren Court's pages have added to the law of this land are new human rights, newly created, newly conceived from the concerned felt and unfelt necessities of our times, to misquote, slightly, Mr. Justice Holmes.

It had never been a human right not to have to go to a separate *but* equal school (now, ironically, there's a demand for a human right to go to a separate *and* equal school).

It had never been a human right to be able to vote regardless of poll taxes or non expertness in state constitutional interpretation, or to be able to eat in a restaurant or buy a house or swim in a park pool regardless of color, or to cast your one vote in an election and in an election district where your one vote counted as much as anyone else's one vote anywhere.

These are not rights spelled out in the Constitution, yet they are implicit in the warp and woof of the assumptions and principles which form its very essence, interpreted as applicable to the time and place of today.

We hear much these days of strict construction and strict construc-tionists. (By way of a footnote, the Warren Court's insistence that each criminal defendant, however indigent, must have the assistance of coun-sel is, if you please, strict construction of the precise words of the Sixth Amendment.)

Strict construction of the Constitution? That yellow document, of erratic spelling and uncertain punctuation, miraculously hammered out by 39 perspiring men in the hot Philadelphia summer of 1787 as a compromise between 13 quarreling little Eastern seaboard states, would not today be the world's oldest living written constitution, governing a complex continent, if it had been constricted by the strict construction for which some now seem to yearn.

The reason that document is still living is that it has been kept living by a Supreme Court alive to the challenge of change and unafraid to infuse new interpretations into the time tested fabric of its fundamental structure.

Surely the confining strait jacket of strict construction would have led in the past, and would lead today, to a wooden rigidity incapable of the flexibility essential to survival in the swirling thrusts of the most dynamic society in history.

In the 180 years of the Supreme Court's history, the 16-year long chapter written by the Warren Court stands out preeminent for its fearless dedication to the never yet reached but always to be fought for ideals of equal rights for all and equal justice for all.

The program, Mr. Chief Justice, lists you as retired. You have not retired and you will never retire from the deep respect and high esteem of your fellow members of The Association of the Bar of the City of New York. That Association, which is honored by having you as one of its few honorary members, is honored to join in honoring you tonight as a great Chief Justice, as a great fighter for the human rights your Court has created, and as a great human being.

Centennial Convocation of the Association of the Bar of the City of New York

Philharmonic Hall, February 17, 1970.

This was the speech in which Francis criticized Richard
M. Nixon for his appointments to the Supreme Court of
Clement F. Haynsworth and George Harrold Carswell,
which subsequently raised such a furor. Chief Justice
Burger, Governor Rockefeller and Mayor Lindsay were
on the stage. Merrell E. Clark introduced Francis to the
assembled Convocation, ending with the words, "It is
fitting that we should soar into our second century with
this man at our head. There is a current advertisement
slogan that goes: "When you've got it, flaunt it." In that
spirit, I present to you our Mr. President, Francis
Plimpton."

This Association's one hundred years is a long time and a short time.
I am not going to take even a short time to deal with that long time,
for I am convinced that the only usefulness of the past is a guide to the
future. You all remember the inscription carved in far off New Deal
days on the Archives Building in Washington—"The Past is Prologue,"
and the answer that Washington taxi drivers used to give to innocent
tourists who asked what it meant: "You ain't seen nothing yet.!"

We have not any of us seen anything yet. It is a truism to point out
that the world in general and this country in particular have changed

more in the last 100 years than in the last 10's of 100's years, and who is to say that it will not change in the next 100 years even faster. Not too long from now we lawyers may well find ourselves feeding states of facts into computers and getting back immediate opinions, or, indeed, judgments. I recall to you the IBM salesman who patted the flank of his block long sample, with its whirling discs and flashing lights and said "Right or wrong, it's always accurate."

As I have said, I will not talk about our last 100 years, for I believe that pride of past all too often leads to a pallid present and a futile future. We *are* proud of our past, even as we admit our short-comings and failures. When the Queen's Bench Division was preparing its annual report to Queen Victoria, the draft read "Your Majesty, conscious as we are of our defects"; Lord Mellish interrupted and said, "Come now, let's be honest—'Conscious as we are of each other's defects'."

From now on I hope we will think of our venerable House on 44th Street, not as the historic landmark which the City of New York has officially decided it to be, but as the launching pad for what we should be doing in our next 100 years.

There is plenty for us to do. Our Constitution says that we were established for the purpose, among others, of "promoting reforms in the law, (and) facilitating and improving the administration of justice."

We *do* reform the law, and we will keep on doing it—for there is a lot to reform. Almost all of the 80 committees of this Association, ranging from the Committee on Administrative Law through those on Housing and Urban Development, Legal Assistance for the Poor, Science and Law, and Uniform State Laws, produce carefully worked out reports, the product of countless hours of dedicated expert hard work, which comment on existing legislation and judicial decisions, approve or constructively disapprove proposed legislation, and suggest reforms in the law—witness our Legal Assistance Committee's recent drastic legislative proposals for the protection of installment financed consumers.

These reports are not trumpeted to the public—the information media are not interested in the non-sensational (their adjective is non-newsworthy), but the committees of Congress and the State Legislature, and, I am glad to say, the Governors of this State—especially the one sitting on this stage—*do* pay attention and *are* guided, steadily and quietly, toward reform of the law.

Somebody once said: "The dogmas of the quiet past are inadequate to the stormy present." The somebody was Abraham Lincoln, and the present he referred to was no more turbulent than is our own.

Are our unobtrusive, calmly analytical committee reports adequate for our stormy present? Do most of them focus on the technique of things as they are and not enough on things as they might be and should be?

Surely the law as an agency of social control is under attack as virtually never before. Violence in and out of court, civil disobedience, lawless contempt for authority, the sullen anger of racial minorities, the disbelief in the existence of justice, all add up to a challenge to our legal institutions which simply cannot be ignored and simply must be faced.

I suppose there are those who would call this Association an association of the Establishment, and I suppose that most of us are, to import a new meaning into what used to be called the longest word in the English language, anti-disestablishmentarians, in that we do believe that our social order should not be torn apart into anarchy, but that it can and should adjust itself, through the orderly processes of law, to the requirements of an ever changing society.

And so I submit that our expert committees should continue to go their hard working expert ways, but that they should be infused, and all our membership infused, with a new sense of urgent and deeply felt concern at the crisis that confronts our legal institutions and law itself, and a new determination, in the long and high tradition of this Association, to seek out and steadfastly fight for the changes that can and should be made to meet the just demands of today and tomorrow. Let us be militant activists, militant activists for the constructive reform of the law we were founded to promote.

What about the second purpose in our Constitution, ''improving the administration of justice''? I shudder to think what a Martian astronaut, seeing for the first time with a fresh and objective eye, would think of our courts and what goes on or does not go on in them. As to the judges, what would he think of certain of them, in theory elected by the public but in fact hand picked by political leaders for purely political purposes irrelevant to merit? All honor to Governor Rockefeller and Mayor Lindsay, both of whom have consulted this Association and other appropriate bar associations before making judicial appointments.

What would our Martian think of Federal appointments? This Association traditionally does not comment on nominations for the bench outside of our areas—obviously we do not have in such cases the means for the searching inquiries we make in our own districts—but I cannot help expressing the wish that the President of the United States' second and third nominees* to the Supreme Court of the United States could have approached, in stature, experience, attitudes and integrity, his first nominee.**

What would our Martian think of certain if not most of the court-houses in this City—antiquated, filthy, noisy, hopelessly over-crowded? What of the incredible delays, delays that mean that criminals can stave off trial for months, if not years, and stave off punishment, by appeals, for years, if not decades? Delays that mean that the innocent victim of a traffic accident may have to wait more than three years before his or her case comes to trial? What of the criminal lack of criminal justice, criminal to the innocent when he has to wait interminably to prove his innocence, and criminal to the public when the guilty can evade so long his punishment?

Our Martian would have to realize that the overall needs of this City are staggeringly monumental—more and better schools, hospitals, police, street cleaning, subways, snow removal equipment for Queens, housing, prisons. The list never ends; City resources do, and choices must be made. But our Martian can well ask whether the prompt and fair administration of justice, civil and criminal, is not the very pre-requisite underpinning of the City itself, and he can well say "You are not doing justice to justice."

And so I think our Martian would say to this Association "You have done much in your first 100 years, but there is much more for you to do in your second. You must see to it that law is relevant to the changing needs and aspirations of all, that there is fair, prompt and impartial justice for all, and that your profession takes the leadership that it should take to make our society a better society over the century to come."

I hope that we will do what he says.

•   •   •

Geoffrey Hellman in his "New Yorker" article tells us in detail the events that followed this speech—in particular the uproar following his

---

*Referring to the nomination of Clement F. Haynsworth and George Harrold Carswell to the Supreme Court.

**Chief Justice Burger.

statement about George Carswell and his nomination to the Supreme Court:

Plimpton's controversial remark, which was greeted with loud and prolonged applause in Philharmonic Hall, was featured in the *Times* the following morning. It was the first public anti-Carswell comment to come from any prominent practicing lawyer. More unexpectedly, it had come from the president of the country's largest and perhaps most influential local bar group. 'Unless, you've lived in the New York City Bar Association,' Samuel I. Rosenman, who has lived in it for forty-seven years and is a former president of it, recently told a lay acquaintance, 'you don't know what an unusual thing that was to say, especially in the presence of the Chief Justice.'

At the time of this unusual remark, Judge Carswell's name had been before the Senate for nearly a month. Among other things, he had been exposed as an incorporator, while United States Attorney in Florida, of a Tallahassee private golf course that had been created from a public, municipally owned, federally financed facility, clearly for the purpose of keeping blacks out, but it still looked as though his confirmation was in the bag: the Judiciary Committee of the Senate had just approved his nomination by a vote of thirteen to four, and the Committee on the Federal Judiciary of the *American* Bar Association had found him "qualified." In the full Senate, where the floor debate on the nomination was soon to start, fewer than twenty members out of one hundred had expressed opposition. In New York law circles, according to Judge Rosenman (a former New York State judge, he is generally known by this title), anxiety about Carswell's qualifications had begun 'in a very submerged kind of fashion.' On an evening exactly a week before Plimpton's controversial remark, Irving M. Engel, a lawyer long identified with civil rights, had called Rosenman up at his home. 'Mr. Engel was distressed about Carswell's golf-club testimony before the Senate committee,' Rosenman says.'He wanted me to do something about it. I started to duck; I don't like to take on outside work these days. [Rosenman, then two days shy of his seventy-fourth birthday, was once special counsel to Franklin D. Roosevelt, and later edited his public papers and addresses.] He said he was going to call some lawyers and ask them to sign a statement opposing the nomination. I said that I wanted to be on the sidelines but that he could use my name. He called me later, and said that he'd talked to three lawyers—Francis Plimpton, Bruce Bromley, and Bethuel M. Webster—and that they had agreed to sign such a statement; would I draw it? [Mr. Bromley, a former judge of New York State's highest court, the Court of Appeals, was a partner in Cravath, Swaine & Moore; Mr. Webster, of Webster, Sheffield, Fleischmann, Hitchcock & Brookfield, was, like Judge Rosenman, a former City Bar Association president.] I got a transcript of the Senate Judiciary Committee testimony. It was very damaging. The more I read, the more incensed I became. I drafted a statement, sent it to the three men on February 13th, and suggested that the four of us sign it. Bromley first said yes, then no, then yes; one of his partners was on the American Bar Association committee that had found Carswell qualified. Beth Webster said yes. I didn't hear from Plimpton. A few days later, at the Centennial Convocation, I congratulated him on his speech, and he apologized for not having had time to read the statement. He called me up the next day and said that he'd sign it. My office got out mimeographs of it [to be precise, a considerably amplified version of the original statement], and we airmailed these around the country to get signatures of prominent lawyers and deans and professors of the leading law schools. We eventually got a total of five hundred and twenty-nine signatures. Early in March, when around four hundred of these had come in, we sent the statement, with the signatures, to every member of the Senate. Our cause at this time looked hopeless. I called up my three original co-signers and said we ought to have a press conference in Washington. The only one who said yes was Plimpton. He was president of the City Bar, but he didn't care.'

The carefree president joined Rosenman at the conference, which was held in the ballroom of the National Press Club on March 12th; the affair was additionally bolstered by the deans of the Harvard and Yale Law Schools and the dean-designate of the Pennsylvania Law School. 'We started all this at a time when it didn't look as though we had a chance to stop Carswell,' Judge Rosenman says. 'The action came at just the right time to lift the morale of those who were fighting. It was very effective. Francis Plimpton was a powerhouse in this. He practically abolished the idea that the president of the Bar Association'—among New York lawyers, this usually means the *City* Bar Association— 'shouldn't mix in political things. He's a very courageous fellow.' (Had Carswell been seated, the Plimpton firm, of course, might have had to plead cases before him.)

On March 17th, the second day of the floor debate in the Senate on the nomination, when the pro-Carswell tide was still running strong, Plimpton, an experienced lobbyist who had been busy trying to line up senators by phone, sent telegrams to *all* the legislators. 'Judge Carswell is not good enough for the Supreme Court, and I devoutly hope that you will vote against confirmation,' he wired, and he went on to place his opposition on legal grounds:

> 'The Court is too important for all of us, and especially for the Congress, to permit any but a highly qualified appointment, and no one, repeat no one, claims that Judge Carswell is highly qualified. [The A.B.A. had simply specified "qualified."] Indeed, the fact that 58% of his appealed-from District Court decisions were reversed—a far greater percentage than normal for district judges—shows anything but judicial competence.'

How much clout did this activity carry? A few days later, Senator Strom Thurmond, of South Carolina, remarked from the floor, 'Like drowning men clutching at straws, the enemies of the nomination point to a charter to a country club.' Not long afterward, one of the drowning men received a rather straw-clutching telegram from Senator Edward J. Gurney, of Florida, a leading Carswell spokesman. It started out, 'You were one of the movers of the petition against Carswell signed by 416 lawyers, and law-school professors,' and it went on:

'The main theme of the petition was that Judge Carswell was an incorporator of a "segregated" private golf
club. *Who's Who* shows that you indicate that you are
a member of the following clubs: Union, Century, Brook,
Downtown, Coffee House, Economic Club, Piping Rock,
Cole [*sic*] Spring Harbor Beach, Metropolitan of Washington and Ausable Cavern [*sic*]. For the record, will
you please advise whether any of these clubs have Negro
members, Jewish members, or Catholic members? If so,
how many, and the approximate date they were admitted
to membership. Thank you for your prompt attention to
this request.'

On the same day, Mr. Gurney sent telegrams similar in
tone to Mr. Plimpton's clubs, asking them whether he—
and, in four interlocking cases, Mr. Webster—was a member; whether the clubs admitted 'blacks, Jews, or Catholics;'
and for their number and approximate date of admission.
(Bromley and Rosenman, whose clubs are not listed in *Who's
Who,* seem to have been spared.)

'The Gurney telegram scared the living daylights out of
the Union Club; I don't think that the Brook answered it,'
the distinguished ten-club clubman said later, but he himself
gave the Gurney request his prompt attention, but at the
same time chose to reply to, the irrelevant *argumentum ad
hominem:*

'Referring to your telegram as to Judge Carswell's
private segregated golf club in Tallahassee, which, while
a United States Attorney, he helped organize . . . I see
no basis for comparison with clubs mentioned in your
telegram. Right to freedom of association in truly private
clubs is required by Federal Civil Rights Act of 1964
Title 42U2. S.Code Annotation Section 2000A (E). The
clubs themselves can tell you of their admission policies,
but I can assure you that I am firmly opposed to any
discrimination as to race or religion anywhere, and that
I personally know Jewish and Catholic members in every
such club, and blacks in the only one to which, so far
as I know, blacks have been proposed for membership.'

During the three weeks of the full Senate debate, the celebrated statement (which had been published *in toto* in the *Congressional Record*) was frequently referred to, and so was its most active disseminator, both pro and con. On the pro side, Senator Clifford P. Case, of New Jersey, said, 'We do not get a Bruce Bromley . . . or a Webster . . . or a Judge Rosenman, or a Plimpton . . . making statements of this sort lightly. Their consciences were outraged by this appointment.' Senator Jacob K. Javits, of New York, remarked, 'When three former presidents [*sic*] of the Association of the Bar of the City of New York, including such traditionalists as Judge Bromley, Francis T. P. Plimpton, and Sam Rosenman, come out against Judge Carswell, it seems to me it is singularly impressive.'' On the con side, Senator Gurney, after referring to a pro-Carswell Yale Law School professor who had worked with the candidate on the establishment of the Florida State University Law School, said, 'This kind of personal working relationship with Judge Carswell impresses me far more than Bruce Bromley and Francis Plimpton and a lot of other attorneys in New York who have had no personal association with or knowledge of the nominee.'

Can the part that the Plimpton-spearheaded legal battalions played in Carswell's 51–45 rejection be precisely evaluated? 'I really believe that had we not done what we did Judge Carswell would now be an Associate Justice of the Supreme Court,' Judge Rosenman wrote Plimpton midway in the Senate debate, and the *Times* has since stated, 'Ultimately, the decisive moving force was the legal profession.' Plimpton himself has summed things up more modestly (and ironically) in the 1969–70 annual City Bar Association President's Report:

> 'Obviously, members of our Association, led by Judge Rosenman, were not solely or primarily responsible for the defeat of the nomination—full credit has to go to President Nixon for his letter telling the Senate that it is supposed to consent and not to advise, and to Senator [Roman L.] Hruska for his stout insistence that there ought to be a mediocrity on the Supreme Court.

But I think that it can be said that the insistence of members of the Association that only excellence belongs on that Court played an important part in the result.'

The Association's president made another attempt at an evaluation in some verses that he read at the Bar Association's annual Twelfth Night Party in 1971:

'Perhaps it really wasn't pain's worth
To worry much about that Haynsworth,

But if you really want some scars, well,
Just think of that High Court with Carswell.

That he's not there's a minor miracle
For which we chant *Te Deums* lyrical

And venture the mild observation
'Twas helped by this Association.'

Well, in any event, the Carswell excursion was, in the light of its genesis, a novelty. 'The Carswell action was one of the first times that the organization of the City Bar said, ''We want quality in the Supreme Court of the United States,'' ' a longtime member of the bar has said. 'It's got up on its hind legs. The episode was a turning point for the Establishment. It meant that the Establishment was getting together to move on things that had hitherto been the province of the non-Establishment.'

Meeting on Military Action in Southeast Asia at the House of the Association—May 19, 1970

The second important action remembered from Francis' years with the City Bar was his organization of the Lawyers' Peace March on Washington to protest the invasion of Cambodia. "The invasion of Cambodia set up a galvanic shock in the New York legal community," he wrote in a Bar Association report. "Does the President of the United States have the right to start a new war? There had been no consultation with Congress or congressional leaders. Secretary of State Rogers had apparently not been consulted. So I was perfectly willing to go along with a meeting in the Bar Association to discuss the whole issue." His first comments on the need for action were in this speech.

I want to start out with a series of disclaimers.

First, I admit to being the President of The Association of the Bar of the City of New York, but I am not, repeat not, here as President, but merely as an individual lawyer representing no one but myself.

Second, this is not, repeat not a meeting of this Association. It is a meeting of members of the Bar, some members of the Association and some not, but all concerned as lawyers with the legal aspects, indeed the legality, of United States military action in Southeast Asia.

This is not, repeat not, a politically partisan meeting. To be sure, there are an inordinate number of prominent Democrats among the 27 sponsors of this gathering. However, there is a non-silent minority of at least 6 registered Republicans, including that stalwart Bruce Bromley and such dubious characters as John Lindsay and myself.

One or two members of this Association have questioned the propriety of a meeting of this sort being held in this House, contending that it is essentially political in character. As President of the Association, I assume full responsibility for this meeting being here, and I will cheerfully face impeachment if the Association feels that I have committed sin. I would point out, however, that the impeachment proceedings should be started promptly, since I expire as President one week from today.

I believe that the doors of this Association should always be open to its members and others who wish to meet here to discuss, as lawyers, the legal issues involved in public controversies no matter how controversial. Surely verbal violence in this room is better than hated violence in the streets, and surely this Association should always welcome those who look at burning issues through the calm eyes of the law and not the inflamed eyes of partisan passion.

I don't know whether it was Talleyrand or Briand or Clemenceau who said "War is too important to be left to the Generals"; I do know that war is too important to be left to the President of the United States.

And I know that it shouldn't be left to him when he seems to have relied solely on the Generals to whom it shouldn't be left either, and apparently not on his Secretary of the Interior or on the leaders of the Senate or the House.

When the President ordered American troops to invade Cambodia, he was acting on his own, in blithe and unilateral disregard of the Congress which under the Constitution has the sole right to declare war and the sole right to raise and support armies (but not to finance them for more than two years at a time), to provide and maintain a navy, and to make rules for the government and regulation of the land and naval forces. But, it will be said, the President is the Commander-in-Chief under the Constitution of the Army and the Navy, and what he did in that capacity didn't involve a declaration of war—he was sending troops not against Cambodia but against aliens using Cambodia as a military sanctuary.

Yet the fact remains that the result of the President's action was a new war, war in another country, war by unilateral Presidential fiat, war without Congressional consultation, without Congressional authorization and without Congressional support. There is no record in American history of any such Presidential presumption—in every single case of American forces going into a foreign country where an immediate emergency was not involved (and almost invariably even then), prior or simultaneous approval of Congressional leaders has been sought and obtained.

There is in the area of the conduct of our foreign affairs, whether carried out by diplomacy or by force of arms, what should be a demilitarized zone between the powers of the President and the power of Congress. I submit that the President has invaded that zone and that Congress should do something about it.

The President has now of course retreated, and stated publicly that American forces will be out of Cambodia by a given date. I do not question his word, or indeed, the genuineness of his desire for peace, but I see no reason why Congress should not back up his word—in fact, give him support against the generals who have so often led us on and on into so many tunnels that turn out to have none of the promised light at the end.

And Congress can give him exactly that support by exercising its undoubted Constitutional right to control the pursestrings, and by providing for specified limitations on appropriations. I hope it will do so.

There are many things that need to be done in this country.

We cannot end poverty overnight.
We cannot end pollution overnight.
We cannot end racial prejudice overnight.
We cannot end inflation overnight.
We cannot end decaying slums overnight.

But we cannot begin to end any of these things until we do end our Southeast Asian folly. Let us get ahead with that ending.

●   ●   ●

I again use Geoffrey Hellman's dramatic version of what happened next, calling Francis Plimpton the most conspicuous participant, if not one of the architects of the Lawyers' Peace March on Washington.

The pilgrims on the next day's march on Washington,
who included associates and partners in virtually all the

leading New York law firms, numbered some twelve hundred,
most of whom occupied nine chartered cars on the 6:30
A.M. train. The rest journeyed by plane, bus and auto-
mobile. 'I am guilty of not going on the train,' Plimpton
says. 'I didn't want to get up that early.' Travelling by plane,
he arrived in time to find his fellow-visitors sitting en masse
on the steps of the Capitol, where a press conference had
been scheduled. 'I arrived at the same time the bullhorn
did,' he says. 'Jack Javits had captured the bullhorn and
was telling how much he was in favor of everything he
should be in favor of. Then Senator Goodell grabbed it and
told how much in favor of the same things *he* was. I grabbed
it and said, "Hello, everybody. Let's go to work." ' The
lobbyists were organized into around a hundred and fifty
teams of six or seven lawyers apiece, each team being
equipped with packets containing the names of the legislators and the State and Justice Department officials to be
visited; lengthy briefing forms; background exhibits; and a
forty-nine-page position paper, with a hundred and forty-
six footnotes, on the legal status of the war. 'My first appointment was with a Southern senator,' Plimpton has related. 'Rain threatened, or it had in New York. I carried
with me my E. J. Korvette umbrella—five ninety-nine plus
tax—which had adhesive tape around the handle inked
"F.T.P.P." The Washington *Post* called it a monogrammed
umbrella. ['He set off briskly across the Capitol grounds,
an urbane figure carrying a monogrammed umbrella,' the
Washington *Post* Service reported in an account that was
syndicated in three hundred and twenty-five papers.] I was
a little late for my appointment. The North Carolina senator
I was to see [Sam J. Ervin, Jr.] was not in his office. He
stood me up. I then went down to the New York Avenue
Presbyterian Church, where Ed Burling and John Douglas
[Edward Burling, Jr., and John W. Douglas, of Covington
& Burling] had assembled a full house—if that's the right
phrase—of Washington lawyers to listen to our New York
story. I talked to them for fifteen minutes on what we were
doing—they were hearteningly responsive. Next, I took my
task force to see the Solicitor General—Erwin Griswold,
former dean of the Harvard Law School and an old friend.

I had a pleasant talk with him. He then arranged for us to see John N. Mitchell, the Attorney General. Mitchell was very polite. I don't think he was carried away, but he did listen to us. I next talked to Elliott Richardson, who was then Under-Secretary of State. He was a fellow-Overseer of Harvard with me. He smokes a pipe. He is one of those superbly deliberate people. He is given to slow sentences. He listened to us with, I hope, understanding.'

What effect did the march have? It was surely not as influential as the Carswell protest: Cambodia was followed by Laos, and the war is still going on. 'I cannot pretend to estimate the impact of this exercise on Washington,' Plimpton told a friend six months later. 'I think it was substantially deeper than the press reports indicated.' In an evaluation that followed his Carswell stanzas at the Twelfth Night Party, the poet Plimpton confined himself to tangential benefits:

'And then it shook you up and snowed ya
When he said 'Invade Cambodia'

Without the least advice congressional,
That feat belongs in his confessional,

But led of course to that famed train ride—
Let no one say it was a vain ride,

For think of all the assist ventral
We gave the ailing old Penn Central,

Postponing for a time, though short,
The embrace of the federal court.'

According to Judge Bernard Botein, presiding justice of the Appellate Division of the New York State Supreme Court and a fellow-marcher, the effect was less easy to pinpoint, but may have been considerable. 'The things that influence legislators are a seamless web,' he says. 'It's not like a Gallup Poll—ever so many intangibles go into the molding of a legislator's policy. I think the peace march was very important because of the character of the people who went on it, led by Plimpton, an impeccable Establishment figure.

There was a good, solid Wall Street turnout. The marchers
were no fringe. They had reasonable haircuts, and they were
largely well dressed, with collars and ties, and, in mary
cases, three-piece suits. This was very impressive to some
congressmen. They hadn't expected it.

New York University Convocation

May 10, 1970

On the occasion of the presentation and dedication of
a bust of Justice Holmes to the New York University Hall
of Fame, Francis received an Honorary LL.D. and made
the following acceptance speech. The ceremonies took
place in the Great Hall of the Bar Association of the City
of New York instead of the Hall of Fame, because of the
student unrest at that time.

I regard this Honorary Degree, as all should regard it, as a tribute, not
to myself, the fleeting President of this Association in its 100th year,
but to the Association itself for its 100 years of dedicated and effective
public service to this City, this State and this Nation.

I am particularly pleased to accept this honored award on behalf of
the Association on this occasion when so many friends are here to pay
tribute to Mr. Justice Holmes, one of the heroes of our profession,
indeed a national hero. The Chief Justice, by his presence here, bears
witness to Holmes' contribution, not only to the life of the law, but to
the welfare of this nation.

And the law does still live. I say that with some assurance, since
last week I sat in this room at the feet, metaphorically, of eminent
scholars presided over by Mr. Whitney North Seymour with the same
urbanity and perspicacity you have witnessed today while he has graced
this occasion. The eminent scholars were discussing, "Is Law Dead?"
Although Whitney did suggest that it was "breathing hard", I am sure
that all who participated in those two days of searching discussion
concluded, Vice President Agnew to the contrary notwithstanding, that

the law is alive and will continue to live if we do not destroy it, in these turbulent times, by our fears and our follies.

I think it is becoming obvious to the silent majority that the most dangerous threats to the life of the law come from the tactics of repression that are urged by some, and not from the spirit of liberty which we cherish in this Hall and in the Hall where this bust will rest.

Neither law nor life was served by putting loaded rifles into the hands of frightened youngsters last Monday.* As we honor the Great Dissenter, we must learn to respect dissent, not because we fear it might become ugly and dangerous, but because of what it may teach us. We of this Association should not be complacently contemplating the achievements of our first 100 years; instead, we should be listening to the dissent of the young, who tell us, if not necessarily like it is, how it looks to fresh and concerned eyes. I hope that we will listen.

---

*A reference to the killings at Kent State.

The Role of Law in World Peace

May 8, 1972

A Speech given at The Association of the Bar of The
City of New York sponsored by the Committee of
International Law before a Symposium composed of
Charles Rhyne, founder of World Peace Through Law
and Philip Jessup, a retired Judge of the World Court

I rise in diffident trepidation. My two colleagues are intimidatingly
better equipped than I am to deal with our topic, The Role of Law in
World Peace. The Judge is not only a former outstanding member of
the International Court of Justice, he is a world authority on international
law and served with unusual effectiveness as a U.S. delegate to the
U.N. in its palmier days; Mr. Rhyne is the dedicated member of our
profession who has done more than anyone else to stimulate lawyers
and judges, worldwide, to strive for world peace through the law.

In the presence of these two, I am doubly hesitant to say what I am
about to say, namely, that if we are interested in world peace in the
here and now we should not be talking tonight about law at all; we
should be talking about something else.

Let me explain what I mean.

Certainly the world is not now at peace. There is a full-fledged war
in Southeast Asia, and the threats to the peace are almost everywhere.
I hope I may be forgiven for mentioning some of them, for if we are
to think about world peace it is just as important to deal with potential
wars before they break out as it is to quench the ones that have started.

First, of course, the Middle East, with Arabs arming, vowing re-clamation by force and refusing negotiation, and Israelis defying United Nations resolutions and clinging to Arab territory acquired by force, not to mention over a million homeless Palestinians sullenly living in refugee camps.

Cyprus, where only a U.N. force keeps ethnic Greeks and ethnic Turks from each other's throats, with disastrous potentials for the tinder of a Middle East already inflammable enough.

Southern Africa, where the challenge to white minority rule over black majorities—in most cases overwhelming black majorities—is a challenge that simmers or boils in Rhodesia, the Portuguese colonies, Southwest Africa and South Africa itself.

The Indian sub-continent, now exhaustedly quiescent, but shaky from religious and racial dissension, possible cross-border intrigue, the Kashmir question and the constant strains of poverty.

Berlin, again at the moment quiet, but always an enclaved hostage to misfortune if and whenever the Communist masters of East Germany choose to make it so.

The Soviet-Chinese border, with some 1,000,000 armed Russians on one side and on the other side growing atomic power and spreading bomb shelters.

Other territorial disputes—the Panama Canal Zone, Alto Adige or Sud Tirol (hopefully now settled); whether you can fish east of the Humboldt Current without being captured by an Ecuadorean or Peruvian gun boat, or fish off Cape Cod with electronic surveillance gear; what are territorial waters and what are territorial sea beds, and who has what rights in the Straits of Malacca and Gibraltar and the narrow entrance to the Baltic Sea?

And the self-baptized wars of liberation, whether sired by Castro, Moscow or Peking, or by one section or party in a country against the rest, and what of outside intervention—Cuban, Soviet, Chinese, British or, if you please, U.S.? What about another Czechoslovakian spring, or another 1956 Hungary, disastrously overshadowed by the Suez folly of Israel, France and Great Britain?

What about the developing countries which welcome or have wel-comed foreign development and investment, and then expropriate it without adequate or any compensation?

What about racial, ethnic and economic discrimination, domestic or international?

I mention this melancholy list of some of the world's difficulties, not as a depressant but as a challenge. What can we do about them, what should we do about them?

It seems to be the assumption of this evening that law should do something about them, and I submit that this is a gross misjudgment of the possibilities and the priorities in the world as it is really today.

What has law to do with the threats to peace I have mentioned? What is the law on Viet Nam? I leave it to those who think that the United States can do nothing that is wrong and those who think it can do nothing that is right, adding the comment that in recent years the latter certainly outshout (if not outnumber) the former.

Where is law in the Middle East? The United Arab Republic signed the U.N. Charter and thereby pledged itself to refrain from aggression or the use of force; Israel also signed that Charter, and thereby pledged itself to obey duly adopted resolutions of the Security Council.

Law in Cyprus? Once it had a lawful Constitution, but who remembers that now?

South Africa ignores the International Court of Justice's advisory opinion that the U.N. has succeeded to the League of Nations' authority over South Africa's mandate over Southwest Africa, and doubly ignores the U.N. resolution taking over that mandate.

The Indian sub-continent? India did promise to hold a plebiscite in Kashmir, the Awami League of East Pakistan did win a majority in the all Pakistan election, the West Pakistan Army did commit partial genocide, India did invade another country. Where is the law?

International treaties supposedly cover Berlin (alas, inadequately and improvidently), Sino-Soviet borders, the Panama Canal and the line between Austria and Italy, but when have those treaties been regarded as the law of the land—the land that doesn't like them? We always thought that there was an international law of the sea, but was it applied by Cairo at Sharm-el-Sheik or by Quito 190 miles west of Guayaquil?

Wars of liberation—can law deal with them? Is the Brezhnev doctrine to be law east of longitude 10° east and is the Monroe Doctrine to be law west of longitude 30° west?

Discrimination? Law has a hard enough time dealing with it in this country, whether racial, ethnic or economic. What about international?

We used to think you could invest in developing the resources of a country that cannot develop them itself and encouraged you to try, and that, if you succeeded (which wasn't by any means always so), you could, under principles of something called international law, count on getting adequate compensation when you were expropriated. Granted the complications of what is adequate (is it what multiple of present earning power, or is it investment plus what rate of return for what risk over the years minus what received, or is it what?), what is now left of that international law? And what is left of oil production agreements that can be reopened (read repudiated) every year or so by one party but not by the other?

I am all too well aware that so far I have sounded like a simplistic hard shell primitive who snorts in disdain at any such concept as a world ruled by law. I do not snort; I can conceive of absolutely nothing as desirable as the 140 odd present nation states irrevocably submitting their differences, whatever they may be, for binding adjudication by a judicial system composed of a Supreme Court of the World with nine impartial and internationally minded justices of the intelligence and integrity of Philip Jessup and Charles Rhyne and, similarly staffed, a Court of Appeals for each continent and a District Court for each region, all applying something fixed and determinable, and enforceable, called international law.

I applaud those who are striving for such a system; I am honored to be a member of an American Society of International Law panel, originally led, and always led in spirit, by Philip Jessup, aimed at strengthening the role and the use of the International Court of Justice, and I devoutly believe in such strengthening; I am sure that Charles Rhyne's conferences quicken the imagination of those who attend them and of those who read what they do.

Yet the fact remains that we are a very, very long way away from any such Supreme Court of the World, or any such fixed, determinable and enforceable international law, and I submit that, while continuing our efforts to attain the millenia, we should make our first order of business the creation, or, if you please, the recreation, of an international mechanism or mechanisms which can deal with threats to the peace not judicially in terms of some non-existent and non-enforceable legal norm, but pragmatically with a view to working out reasoned compromises of conflicting claims and interests.

Natural law means one thing in Madrid and another thing (if anything at all) in Moscow, and still other things in New Delhi, Djakarta, Peking and Tokyo; it does little good to preach Grotius to the Peruvian Navy or the Declaration of Human Rights to Pretoria.

What would do good is for the White House and the Kremlin, not to argue as to who is lawful and who isn't, or as to what court and what law should govern, but for them to engage in constant and repeated conferences and negotiations as to what their differences are, as to how some of them can be composed or compromised, and as to how the other can be minimized or postponed.

What would do good is for the countries that do want to fish world-wide—the U.S., Japan and the Soviets, for example, not to argue a non-agreed-to law of the sea, but to sit down with Ecuador and Peru, to recognize how economically dependent those two are on the catch leagues off their shores, and to come to some reasonable limitation on foreign use of those waters or reasonable compensation for such use—all without admitting coastal sovereignty for any other purpose beyond heretofore agreed upon limits.

What we hope will do good is for Bhutto and Indira Gandhi to negotiate out their difficulties—more good, I believe, than would result from any attempt by either or by any outsider to submit those differences to some non-existent law.

There isn't any law about Swiss, French and German pollution of the Rhine and the effect on the Netherlands and Belgium, and any such law isn't around the corner; what should be around the corner is a conference of those countires and a negotiated Rhine agreement between them.

In short, I think our strongest efforts should be concentrated, not on promoting a hoped for but far-off world ruled by law, but on the imperative and immediate necessity of more and better bilateral and multilateral negotiation and solution by negotiation—more and better diplomacy.

Now the word "diplomacy" has an old-fashioned sound redolent of Metternich, dancing and Vienna, although it should be remembered that the peace produced by that Congress lasted virtually intact for almost 100 years. Needless to say, I do not mean socializing in striped pants, a process which I doubt ever existed (in some five years at the U.N., I saw only one pair—which *was* from Vienna); I do mean the constant and continued effort by trained and knowledgeable experts to deal with present and foreseeable threats to the peace by persistent negotiation and persistent search for bargained agreement.

So far I haven't mentioned the pre-eminent forum for international negotiation and diplomacy, the United Nations. Now the U.N. is not in particular favor these days, partly because of its peacekeeping failures and partly because of its own structure (one nation one vote in the Assembly) and ineptitudes—financial and operational. One can under-stand American resentment against the expulsion of Taiwan; however, the membership had to choose between only two realistic alternatives: keeping Taiwan, which meant Peking would not come in, and expelling Taiwan and bring Peking in; that there were only such two alternatives is partly our own fault for having opposed Peking's entry so long, and one can't blame the members (many of them our best and most knowledgeable friends) who thought it of primary importance to get Peking in, despite the possible injustice to Taiwan. Also, why can't the U.S. be a good loser?

The fact that the U.N. Security Council, on account of the veto, cannot take any step which is disapproved of by the Soviet Union, China or ourselves, not to mention Great Britain and France, and the fact that General Assembly resolutions (which in fact are no more than recommendations) can be passed by a two-thirds vote of Afro-Asians and Communists, should not make us forget what unparalleled opportunities those East River glass houses offer for diplomacy and negotiation—the whole world at our doorstep.

One of the outstanding examples is in a sense on this platform: it was in the U.N. delegates' lounge that U.S. delegate Philip Jessup picked up a remark by Soviet delegate Jacob Malik and pursued and developed it into the negotiations that led to the end of the Berlin blockade and airlift.

So even if the U. N. can't solve the Middle East and Viet Nam, and even if some of the member governments won't pay their bills and talk far too much and pass meaningless resolutions, surely it is worth our while to pay less than the cost of the New York City Fire Department to support and keep at our doorstep the ideal place for us to engage in what I believe to be the present best hope of the world for peace—diplomacy and negotiation.

PART FOUR

Population
And
Education

Population and Education

In his role as ex-diplomat, president of the City Bar and a member of the House of Delegates of the American Bar Association, Francis made many speeches which tell us what he thought about the important issues of this time. To mention a few: he gave the address at the Alumni Spread of the Harvard Law and Graduate Schools (1965); the Root Lectures at the Council of Foreign Relations in 1967, called "Reflections on a Glass House" in three parts, and a speech before the Chicago Council of Lawyers (1970). In his words, "it was a newly-formed group of younger lawyers in revolt against the Chicago Bar Association who invited me as a supposed liberal ally." He also addressed the National Bar Presidents in Montreal (1975), the Fiftieth Anniversary of his Harvard Law School class, and was greatly honored to be asked to give the Morrison Lecture to the 1977 Annual Meeting of the State Bar of California. (The Chief Justice, the Honorable Rose Elizabeth Bird, made her remarks in light verse!)

Francis carried a small, black, invaluable notebook in his pocket in which he kept all kinds of information, from lists of friends to invite to dinner to the sizes of his sons' shirts, along with a series of jokes. He would have been lost without it. When he was thinking about a speech, he would consult it to find a funny story appropriate for the occasion. He liked to lighten the atmosphere before proceeding to the serious part.

For instance, he once introduced the Archbishop of Canterbury at a Folger Shakespeare Library function telling this story: "There was a discussion going on in the House of Commons about the Church of England. Suddenly, a back-bencher shouted 'Stand fast by the Church of England, it's our only defense against Christianity!' " The Archbishop took it in good part and said that he would have to use that one himself.

In his early years, Francis used to speak from a few notes, extemporaneously, but after his United Nations experience and the presidency of the City Bar, he would write them out and have prepared copies.

One of the topics that particularly concerned him was population control.

In fact, the first contretemps Francis had with the State Department was over a speech on Planned Parenthood he had promised to give at the anniversary dinner of the Planned Parenthood Federation of America in the fall of 1961—a speech still remembered.

It never occurred to him to have this speech cleared at the State Department, until one evening, riding back with Richard Gardner from a conference at the American Assembly, Francis showed him the speech he was planning to give. Gardner, who was on the U.N. desk of the State Department at that time, was horrified and told him he couldn't possibly give this without having it cleared. The speech accordingly was sent down to Washington where it went all the way up to the White House. Francis was furious at the cuts that were made—every mention of the Catholic Church was taken out, for instance. He was almost about to resign. Harlan Cleveland, then Assistant Secretary for International Organizations, called him about it. Francis protested vigorously, saying he was giving this speech in his private capacity. Cleveland replied, "Now, Francis, suppose you were picked up drunk in the gutter at Times Square, taken to the station house, and a policeman said, 'Why Ambassador Plimpton!' Are you acting in a private or public capacity?" Francis subsided and admitted afterwards that the third that was cut from the speech improved it by making it shorter. Here are excerpts, making it even shorter. He called it "Population, the U.N. and the U.S."

> I first want to make it clear that I am speaking entirely as a private citizen and not in an official capacity. What I may have to say represents nothing but my own personal views and convictions, and not those of a New Frontiersman, even if a somewhat staid New York lawyer, now thinly disguised as a diplomat, could ever qualify for that dashing sobriquet.
>
> I warn you not to be disappointed—when anyone disavows officialdom, he is expected to be pleasantly indis-

creet, particularly when the topic verges on that delectable subject, sex. I remind you in this connection of the well-known comparison between two topics—the weather and sex. As to the weather, everyone talks about it but nobody does anything about it. As to sex—the reverse is true. However, I *am* going to talk, if not about sex, about its product—population.

I am sure you expect me to start with the ringing phrase "Population Explosion," but I am going to do no such thing, principally because there is no such thing. I will admit that there has been a population explosion at the United Nations, where the number of members has almost doubled in the last ten years, but I would hasten to add that neither I nor anyone else advocates birth control for U.N. membership. The United States, as the very first anti-colonialist power, the very first dependent country to become independent, welcomes the thrust of other peoples for their own independence, welcomes the upswelling surge for self-determination (whether in Africa, Asia or Berlin), and welcomes the newly independent nations to full participation, as sovereign equals, in the world's meeting place that is the United Nations.

I have said there is no such thing as a population explosion. Explosion connotes a sudden, blasting shock, a single shock, one which does its damage, but which, once over like a thunder clap, is finished. That is not what our population problem is. To be sure, it is a problem the realization of which has burst upon us like a star shell, as the spectacular scientific increase in control over death, without any corresponding increase in control over birth, has resulted in burgeoning net population growth. But the graphs that we all see, with their sharply climbing lines that mount upwards to the upper-right hand corner of the page, do not come to an end and are not going to. There is no explosive asterisk at the end of the line, no little miniature, star-shaped symbol to indicate that there has been an explosion, that the damage has been done, and that we do not need to worry about it any more. The line doesn't stop—it keeps going on, and it keeps going up.

The truth is that the population problem is one that is

going to be with us for years, one that cannot be dealt with in the convulsive connotation of an explosion. We Americans sometimes think that the problems of the world can be solved by brisk and impulsive crash programs, announced ahead of time by the bugles of Madison Avenue, and pushed with the strident self-righteousness of self-appointed world saviorism.

I invite anyone who believes that this approach will work in the world of today to visit the Institution on the East River where I spend my waking hours. The visitor will find there in microcosm the whole varying diversities of the world's peoples, races, cultures and societies, and the whole bewildering complexities of the world's problems—most of them insoluble, or presently so, or they would not be there.

In this world frame of reference, and that is the world that *does* frame us, no problem, and least of all the population problem, can be treated as a simple, unitary and momentary difficulty which will meekly succumb to a good strong dose of American energy and American common sense. So I urge you, in your thinking of and dealing with the world's population explosion, *not* to be explosive, but to be thoughtful, tolerant (but not tolerant of intolerance), patient, hopeful of prompt results but, regardless of lack of progress or misunderstanding, steadfastly determined to make the world realize the full implications of the present flooding rate of population growth.

Even if one cannot properly say that there is a population explosion, certainly there has been a publicity explosion of public interest in the population problem.

I need hardly remind you of last April's hard-hitting speech by Eugene Black, President of the World Bank, before the U.N. Economic and Social Council, in which he said that he was "increasingly doubtful whether domestic savings and foreign aid together will be sufficient to allow real progress, if present rates of population growth continue for long," and further said, "I must be blunt. Population growth threatens to nullify all our efforts to raise living standards in many of the poorer countries."

You all know the definition of an optimist as a man who is learning Russian and a pessimist as a man who is learning

Chinese. Mr. Black's definition, in the same speech, is more down to earth. He said:

> "We are coming to a situation in which the optimist will be the man who thinks the present living standards can be maintained. The pessimist will not even look for that. Unless population growth can be restrained, we may have to abandon for this generation our hopes of economic progress in the crowded lands of Asia and the Middle East."

So we do have a *new* problem to deal with, and not one that we can rely on the experience of the past to solve for us.

I do not ask tonight the fateful question as to whether the fertility of the soil can catch up or keep up with the fertility of man—but I note in passing that Communist China's great leap forward has turned into a faltering stumble as regards feeding her own teeming millions; the question I do ask is whether any less developed country can expect any real economic development in the face of inordinate and untrammeled population growth.

And let there be no mistake—the under-developed countries of the world must largely depend on their own excess productivity, their own savings, if they are to achieve continuing economic development and industrialization. The United States is proud that it pioneered the concept of initial capital assistance from the more developed countries to the less, and it will continue to do its share, but all students of the problem agree that the bulk of the needed resources for continuing economic development must come from savings within the country itself. And if these savings have to be used in a desperate struggle to provide for the elementary needs of an exploding population, there will be no continuing economic development. Human over-reproduction means economic underproduction.

Our realization of the population problem is cumulative. Two generations ago the unwanted child was a tragedy for the health of the mother. A generation ago it was realized that the unwanted child was a tragedy for the economic health of the family. We now realize that the unwanted child may well be a tragedy for the economic health of an entire people. Perhaps we will soon realize that the unwanted child may be a threat to the economic health of the whole world.

In these days of the equality of women (and the superiority of children) I hope you will not think that I am looking at these problems too much from the male standpoint. You will remember, in this connection, the lady who decided to go into the poultry business and ordered 25 hens and 25 roosters. One of her male neighbors, on visiting the chicken yard, commented that she did not need 25 roosters and that two would have been enough. "Oh," she said, "that's only a man's viewpoint."

And the Supreme Court of the United States has spoken, albeit in a somewhat confused and discordant chorus of voices, as to the Connecticut statute which purports to regulate conduct in that most unregulatable of locations, bed. The opinion of the majority of the Court, blindfolded in the best tradition of all court house statues of justice, resolutely shuts its eyes to the very existence of the statute; the customary spate of dissents again indicates that constitutional law is not exactly an exact science.

You have also read that the indications are that Latin America will have to double its income in the next thirty years simply to maintain already low standards of living. Let us hope that Latin America will not be turned into that country of the Red Queen in Alice's *Through the Looking Glass* "where it takes all the running you can do to stay in the same place."

One sometimes hears it said that population growth is an old problem, old since Malthus in 1798, that it has always solved itself, and that we need not worry about a situation that will work itself out.

There are two troubles with this viewpoint—first, that the problem's own solutions have been epidemics, famine and war, apocalyptic solutions that are not exactly welcome today, and second, that the problem today is virtually a *new* problem.

It is new because of the sudden and massive impact of the services of modern medicine and modern public health on the death rate of countries which until recent times had very high mortality untouched by any such services. With the birth rate remaining the same, the obvious and necessary result has been an explosive increase in population.

Take Ceylon, where a recent public health program, based in part on the spraying of DDT on malarious areas at a cost of some 14 cents a head, resulted in 10 years in cutting the death rate in half, with of course no change in the birth rate. The resulting population bulge was and is inevitable.

It is ironical that as regards the great ultimate mysteries of life we know more about its end, death, than we know about its beginning, conception. Surely our research organizations should probe into what brings us into this world as well as into what takes us out of it, for with the answer we would be able to make this a better world for us to come into.

I have tried to deal with the governmental implications of population problems. What are they for those of us in this room and the other members of your Planned Parenthood Federation? I think there are two.

First, I adjure you to keep up your good work and to raise your sights. Your clinics *should* number the thousands, your educational material *should* reach millions that want it; your research program *should* be commensurate with the stubborn challenge of the problem it seeks to solve. Just as economic productivity must outmarch reproductivity, so must your productivity climb faster and higher than the uprising line that disappears into the upper right-hand corner of your charts.

Finally, I urge upon you cooperation and I recall to you the story told by the late Thomas W. Lamont about his father, a Presbyterian minister in upstate New York. The local Catholic priest was fond of coming and sitting on the parsonage porch and discussing theological matters. In the cool of the evening he would always depart, saying, "Good-bye, Riverend Lamont. We will both be about God's work, you in your way and I in His."

Surely the problem of finding a solution for the world's exploding populations, exploding in the very areas where

some balance between reproduction and production is essential to physical and economic health and progress, is one
to challenge the best that is in all of us, Catholic, Jew,
Protestant, Muslim, Buddhist, Western and Eastern.

Surely here is a New Frontier toward which all of us
can march together, united in our determination to make a
better world for all peoples.

This chapter on population would not be complete without Francis'
story of his encounter with the Pope, Pope Pius XI:

In the summer of 1963, just before we were to fly to
Italy for our yearly visit to a Villa we had on Lake Como,
I was waited on by Ambassadors to the U.N. from Ceylon,
Nepal and Cambodia. At the time, Diem was still President
of South Vietnam and there was a good deal of talk about
Catholic persecution of Buddhists. The Ambassadors wanted
me to ask President Kennedy to intercede with the Pope on
the matter.

It occurred to me that I had never met a Pope and that
this would be a good excuse. So I wrote ahead to our
Embassy in Rome to arrange an interview, saying I would
like to discuss Catholic persecution of Buddhists in Vietnam
and population problems. I threw in the population idea for
my wife, who served on various Planned Parenthood Boards,
and was very much interested. We stopped off in Rome,
staying at the American Academy with the then President,
Richard A. Kimball.

To our surprise the appointment had been made for the
next day. I borrowed a black tie from Dick Kimball and
went off to Castel Gandolpho with someone from the Embassy as escort. We went up in a rickety elevator, the Swiss
Guards presenting halberts as we passed through various
ante-rooms to the private library of the Pope. A Nigerian
and his very fat wife in elaborate dress were both backing
out of the room as we waited to enter.

The Pope had an interpreter, but we talked in French,
mine battered but his fluent and heavily accented, which
made it easier to understand. I started right in on Catholic
persecution in Vietnam: he was quite defensive and said

that he had urged them to be 'raisonable', a curious word to use. Indeed, the next day, the Rome newspapers said that he had remonstrated with Diem as to the repression of Catholics. I then said that the U.N. was much interested in population problems and that I hoped the Pope would use his influence on Catholic countries not to object. His Eminence was absolutely inflexible; his face froze and he said that you could not change Divine Law and he used the phrase "tuer la vie humane" and that it was a matter for FAO (Food and Agricultural Organization). Consequently, I was not a bit surprised at his adamant position on birth control and his opposition to any discussion in the U.N. of population problems. The interview lasted a little over half an hour. I've been kidded ever since for trying to convert the Pope to birth control.

● ● ●

Often asked to give Commencement addresses, Francis invariably used these occasions to educate his listeners about the United Nations and its problems. Here is the graduation speech he gave at Smith College in the spring of 1962.

Mr. President, members of the Class of 1962, proud parents, ladies and gentlemen:

I have a Smith wife and a Smith mother-in-law, I had a Smith stepmother, and I have a Smith daughter, a Smith daughter-in-law, and a Smith niece. You Seniors have finished your Smith education—I am in the middle of mine, and hope that I will never finish it.

In my uneasy anguish over what to talk to a female graduating class about, I asked a friend of mine for advice— a Bryn Mawr girl, by the way, just to show that I can occasionally escape from unadulterated Smithhood.

Her advice was simple: remember that you're talking to women, and don't behave like every other Commencement speaker who lectures sweet girl graduates as though they were about to leave the Carnegie Institute of Technology for a career of public service in engineering with the Tennessee Valley Authority.

I was forced to remind her of the historic and well-known episode in the French Chamber of Deputies years ago when a proponent of women's suffrage summed up his argument by saying, "After all, there is very little différence between men and women," whereupon, as you all know, the Chamber rose as one man and cried, "Vive la différence!"

You are now about to become alumnae. I hope that you will not think that because you are alumnae you have completed your education. We are all familiar with the spate of books that have been cascading from eminent educators, from President Conant on down, all bewailing the state of American education. I do not disagree with these strictures, although I am inclined to think that the flooding pressures for admission are forcing up the standards of under-graduate performance to heights that would have dismayed my generation—witness the thankfulness of your parents, and of myself, that we got into college when we did and got out when we did.

I would join in bemoaning our shortcomings in scientific education. I remember with apprehension a visit a few years ago to a boarding school in the outskirts of Leningrad, where I saw eager red-cheeked blond 12-year-olds, boys and girls together, avidly learning physics.

But I bemoan even more than American education's shortcomings its short going. Far too often the opening of diplomas means the closing of books, the urge to learn fades into the urge to earn, and graduation is only *from* and not *to*. I know of no more mournful sight than the American college graduate, male or female, whose education stopped at commencement—stopped, mind you, at the very point—commencement, when it should commence all over again.

Perhaps in point is an unpublished couplet by that superb member of the Amherst faculty, one Robert Frost:

"So now there's education for adults,
For those who had it once—without results."

From now on you must educate yourselves. Here at

Smith you have had the inestimable benefit of good teaching,
but in the last analysis there is no such thing as good teaching—there is only good learning. Here you have had the
stimulus of supervision; from now on you will need the
stimulus of inner vision. Many of you have found a Smith
College education a tough and demanding business; I warn
you that your self-education may require even greater resources of inside strength.

I say "may" because in fact self-education ought to be
the easiest of educations. We are all familiar with Mar-
quand's alumnus (of Harvard, please, not Amherst) who
would fitfully try to salve his educational conscience by
attempting to read Gibbon's "Decline and Fall of the Roman
Empire," and inevitably, after a few pages, would himself
decline and fall into guilty sleep.

That is not the kind of hair shirt self-flagellation I mean
by self-education.

What I mean is what happens when a lively mind, alert
and avid for new knowledge and fresh insight, is self-im-
pelled into spirited inquiry and keen analysis, into the high
adventure of exploring the unexplored frontiers of the world
today. I would remind you of Thoreau's saying that a frontier
is "neither west nor east, but wherever a man (I add, or a
woman) faces a fact."

Surely every one of you Seniors in facing that kind of
a frontier has experienced the inner leap of intellectual curiosity, the compulsive urge to find an answer and the rapture,
careful rather than careless, that comes when you do find
it.

Surely *you* have learned that learning is fun, and that
exercising your mental muscles produces an inward glow
even more satisfying than the outward glow that follows a
row on Paradise Pond.

This being so, why should there be any worry about
your continuing your education, about your self-education?

The trouble is, of course, that the Smith world is full
of one thing—education (except, of course, on week-ends,
when an Amherst man always thinks it's full of Yale men)—
whereas the world you are commencing into is full of a
number of things—an unnumberable number of things.

It is full of husbands, children, careers, politics, the stock market (lamentably so), bridge, budgets, the twist, foreign affairs, golf, astronauts, sweet peas, existentialism, automation and the 12-tone scale.

Here you have benefitted from what, to paraphrase Thorstein Veblen, might be called the leisure of the theory class; from now on you will find your hours crowded with the multiplicities of a world where complexity seems to multiply with each morning's newspaper.

This means that you will have to discriminate. "Discrimination" is a nasty word racially, but it is a proud word as applied to the wise and discriminating choice of the possible from the impossible and of the worthwhile from the meretricious.

I sound as though I were saying that, abandoning all else, you must solemnly dedicate 1 hour and 15 minutes a day to a separate and distinct exercise known as self-education. That is not what I mean, although I suspect that the exercising of your mental muscles will often be pleasanter than 18 exasperating holes at your country club or 4 exacerbating rubbers in your drawing room.

What I do mean is that your crowded hours should not be so crowded as to crowd out learning, to crowd out the acquisition of knowledge, in short, to crowd out self-education.

For knowledge *is* power, what you don't know *will* hurt you. Knowledge as to anything, whether it is the Italian bidding system or real estate values or mental hygiene or dress design or the Common Market or fluoridization *does* matter. You as women, as wives and mothers and executives and artists and writers and scientists and politicians and just plain human beings, *matter,* and what you do know and don't know *matters*, and matters decisively.

All of this sounds as though I were urging you all to hurry up and join the League of Women Voters. I do indeed, for surely you should be in a position to instruct your husbands and other admirers as to the issues before the country and as to how they should vote on them.

However, I would also urge you to join the Daughters of the American Revolution. I have no sympathy with those

who poke easy fun at DAR bosoms and bouquets, or with
those who resign because of disagreement with their resolutions. I believe in the DAR's deep patriotism and love of
country, but I also believe that true patriotism must be based
not only on love of country but on love of truth and the
facts.*

I cannot believe that the DAR resolutions against the
United Nations and the United States participation in the
United Nations Bond Issue can be based on anything except
a misunderstanding of truth and of the facts, and I cannot
think of any more useful purpose to which your education
and self education could be put than to make known the
truth and the facts about the U.N. and its affairs not only
to the DAR but to others who, it seems to me, behave like
the young lawyer who said to the Court, "These are the
conclusions on which I base my facts."

I am afraid that the passers of resolutions against the
U.N. are relying on statements like that made by General
Edwin Walker, who is reported to have said that "Dag
Hammarskjold was a Red Swede who took his instructions
from Moscow." I have no doubt that General Walker is a
patriotic and first-class soldier, but there could be no greater
or more flagrant calumny against a gallant and intrepid international civil servant who, bitterly denounced and opposed by the Soviets, gave his very life for international
peace.

The passers of resolutions against the U.N. seem to be
under the impression that with its changed membership and
one vote per country, the United States is being pushed
about and led around by the nose to the detriment of its
national interests. It *is* true that of the 104 members, 52 are
from Africa or Asia, and that the Republic of Gabon with
some 400,000 inhabitants has the same one vote that the
United States does with 180,000,000.

I remind you, by the way, that in the United States
Senate, Nevada, with some 285,000 inhabitants, has the
same two votes that New York does, with 16,800,000, and

---

*Francis got several indignant letters about this paragraph, taking him to task
for seeming to approve of the DAR and ignoring the next paragraph.

that with, to be sure, some assistance from the House of Representatives, our country survives—although I would remind you of Theodore Roosevelt's request of Carl Akeley that he bring back from Africa a couple of lions to be turned loose in the Senate. "But," asked Akeley, "aren't you afraid they would make a mistake?" "No," said T.R., "not if they stayed there long enough."

I have always been struck by the irony involved in a college commencement. You finish, and having finished, you commence. I suppose that is as it should be—in the continuum that is the stream of our lives every end is a beginning, every finish a commencement. You have finished your stay under these lovely elms and in these quiet quadrangles and now you commence your journey from this smiling valley into the world outside. May you carry with you what this College has given you, high standards, intellectual integrity, love of the truth and devotion to the best that is in you. God speed you on this, the commencement of your journey.

PART FIVE

Pro Bono Publico

Pro Bono Publico

Americans who have successful careers seem to feel an obligation to Society as a whole. Francis was a particular exemplar of this. Very often, it was an honor as well as a duty—his pro bono publico activities. He served on the Boards of his school, Exeter, of his college, Amherst, of Barnard, Athens College in Greece, Lingnan University in China and the Union Theological Seminary and was an Overseer of Harvard (though an Amherst man) for the six years, 1963–1969. In the banking world, he was a Trustee of the United States Trust Company and the Bowery Savings Bank. His hospital Board was Roosevelt.

He was a Trustee of TIAA (Teacher's Insurance and Annuity Association), Chairman of the Trustees of TIAA stock and the President of the members of CREF (College Retirement Equities Fund), serving in these various positions from 1949 until his retirement in 1975. CREF was the first variable annuity company organized to invest pensions of colleges and their staff members in common stock to provide a chance to share in the growth of the economy. I remember once when we were visiting Lloyd's of London, we were invited into the inner sanctum to have tea with a vice president. To make conversation, I brought up Francis's connection with insurance and made Francis describe the idea behind CREF. The vice president of Lloyd's had never heard of such a plan!

As to the Arts, he was a director of the Philharmonic Symphony Society of New York, and the Metropolitan Museum of Art, Chairman of the Egyptian Committee. As an Ambassador, he helped the Museum obtain the Temple of Dendur. He was President of The Century Association for five years, 1968 through 1972, afterwards described in a resolution of the Board of Management as *The Age of the Plimpton Enlightenment*. After leaving the U.N., he kept on with his international interests as a member of the Council of Foreign Relations, the Foreign

Policy Association and the Academy of Political Science of which his father had been one of the Founders. He was a Director of the U.N. Association of the U.S.A., a President of the Federation of French Alliances, Chairman of the American Ditchley Foundation and a Vice President of the America-Italy Society, to name a few.

One of his pleasantest associations was being a Vice President of U.I.A. (Union Internationale des Avocats), the world's oldest International Bar Federation, founded by lawyers from France, Belgium and Luxembourg in 1927. At the 1971 Biennial Meeting in Paris, he had been presented with the Medal of the Ville de Paris at an impressive ceremony at the Hotel de Ville.

When asked to be President of the U.I.A., he felt he had done his share and declined. His younger partner, Harold H. Healey, Jr. went on to become the first President of the U.I.A. from the United States. The biennial meeting of the U.I.A. in 1981 was held in New York. Francis was instrumental in having them entertained by the Mayor and at the House of the Association of the Bar of the City of New York. But the most inspired event was the first meeting held in the General Assembly Hall of the United Nations. We ourselves had the Governing Body, forty strong, with their wives for a meeting and lunch in the country. He was proud of the way we held up our end without the governmental support given by other countries.

I once asked a member of a Board about how important it was for him to attend all of the meetings to which he went so assiduously. I gathered that his contribution was substantial and valued. Two stories have come to me as to how he contributed. When Francis was a Trustee of the Union Theological Seminary, John N. Irwin II was President during the turbulent times of the sixties. He asked Francis to come and be by his side at an open Board meeting demanded by students who felt that the Seminary should give forty per cent of its endowment to Black Power. After the impassioned speeches by the students, Jack Irwin turned to Francis as his legal counsel for aid. Francis stood up and said, "I have only two things to say: one, it would be illegal; two, it would be immoral" and sat down. His words and the conviction with which he said them ended the turmoil.

The other story concerns Amherst, and I quote former President William Ward, who considered Francis to be the ideal trustee:

> On one occasion, college officials knew they had to
> inform the trustees of an odd legal exception that might have

allowed the college to avoid paying thousands of dollars in legal damages. Mr. Plimpton leaned forward and said quietly, "The Trustees of Amherst College would never invoke a legal technicality to protect themselves against their fiduciary responsibility." When the discussion continued, Plimpton ended it, saying quietly but firmly, "I do not want to hear the fact raised again."

It was fitting that when Francis was drawn into the affairs of the City of New York he was appointed Chairman of the Board of Ethics by Mayor Lindsay. He was also made Chairman of the Mayor's Commission for Distinguished Guests by Mayor Beame in 1976 and was sometimes teased about being a modern Grover Whalen. He was very proud about the chairmanship of the Board of Ethics, which he felt was a great honor. The Board gives advice to City officials and other employees as to what they may or may not do under the City's Code of Ethics. The Board has no subpoena powers, but to quote Francis: "Quaintly, I find that City employees and others faithfully follow our decisions and do what we say and almost without exception do not do what we tell them not to do. Even the Mayor has been good enough to acquiesce in some of our unpopular decisions."

Francis liked working in the historic City Hall and with the people there with whom he came in contact. He always would try to turn up at the Mayor's receptions so that he could get to know the members of the City Administration better. People sometimes criticize our City Government and its bureaucracy, but I never heard Francis do so.

There was one incident which did infuriate him. The City car which was supposed to take him to meet Prince Charles coming in on a British helicopter to the Wall Street Heliport was delayed. In his haste, the driver couldn't find the right ramp to leave the Expressway, and Francis, late, got out of the car, crossed the center guard rail and climbed over the railing to get there on time. I shudder at the thought of what might have happened and was glad to see that the *Paris Herald* had a picture of Francis greeting Prince Charles on its front page!

Francis was given the Bronze Medal of the City of New York in 1975. In 1983 Mayor Koch presented him with the Fiorello H. La Guardia Award. The ceremony was held in the historic Board of Estimate room. Every seat was taken. When the Mayor saw the number of people assembled which was not usual on such occasions, his only comment was "Wow!" Francis's acceptance speech was the last that he made except for standing to give the Loyal Toast, "The Queen," at a dinner of The Pilgrims of the United States. The Mayor introduced Francis, saying in his speech that "Francis Plimpton is only the fourth person to receive the La Guardia Medal, for the yardstick of individual accomplishment is very special indeed."

Francis rose to reply: (in part)

I notice that the Mayor has dignified me with the title of "Honorable." It is a good many years since, as an ambassador, I was entitled to the sobriquet. If anyone mentions the time-honored aphorism "Once an ambassador, always an ambassador," I remind you of Evita Peron, the beautiful wife of the late dictator of the Argentine, who had a somewhat dubious provenance. She was riding around in an open car in Madrid when the crowds unfortunately yelled at her "puta," "puta." I need hardly recall to this distinguished audience that "puta" is the most unfortunate noun that can possibly be applied to a woman. The Spanish grandee sitting next to her patted her on the shoulder and said, "Senora, you must not be surprised, I resigned from the army 20 years ago and still they call me 'general'."

I feel particularly honored by receiving a LaGuardia Medal. I remember very well in 1933, when I was the General Solicitor of the Reconstruction Finance Corporation, being deputized by the Board of Directors to go up to Capitol Hill and testify before the Interstate Commerce Committee of the House of Representatives, chaired by none other than Fiorello La Guardia. In fear and trembling, I proceeded to a hearing attended by a considerable number of reporters, avid to record the expected humiliation. To my astonishment, Fiorello's questions, although searching and very much to the point, delivered in his high-pitched combination of Prescott, Arizona, and lower East Side accent, were quite temperate. Fortunately, neither he, nor needless to say, I, asked any questions as to our ill-fated attempt to rescue the Van Sweringen railroad empire. The net result was that I went back to the RFC battered but unbowed, with a profound respect for Fiorello La Guardia.

It has been a pleasure to have been of any service to his

City. I have thoroughly enjoyed the job of Chairman of the Mayor's Commission for Distinguished Guests.

It was fun watching the Ghanian band, with its leopard-costumed drummers, greeting the President of Ghana in the wastes of JFK where his air force plane landed, but it was not so much fun being jostled and trampled by the hundreds of Ghanian citizens who were anxious to show their loyalty by being the first to greet him. I will never forget Mayor Beame's and my visit to the Waldorf Astoria Towers prepared to present the Key of the City to the President of Nigeria, when we found ourselves engulfed in a horde of reporters who, it turned out, had no intention of recording our visit, but were only intent on getting an interview with Bob Hope about the death of Bing Crosby.

It has been fun to greet a varied collection of dignitaries, ranging from arrogant Prime Minister Begin, charming Francois de Laboulaye, the last French Ambassador to this country, Washington born and educated, the affable Prince of Wales and the attractive English speaking King and Queen of Sweden.

Most of all, I have enjoyed the meetings of the various dignitaries with the Mayor. He has handled them superbly, with verve, wit and humor, the very model of what a Mayor should be. Working with him and for the City is a pleasure I shall always remember.

PART SIX

Epilogue

Epilogue

On September 30, 1983, two months after his death, an astonishing number of Francis' friends gathered in his honor at the Madison Avenue Presbyterian Church. The mellow voice of Dr. David H. C. Read and the music of Bach and Brahms, which Francis would have loved, rose up over the people in the great church. The contributions that were made were tributes to different phases of his career—a summary and a celebration of his life and service.

First, George N. Lindsay, one of Francis' law partners, who has told me that he joined the firm because of meeting Francis, went to the pulpit, and said as follows:

> For some fifty years, Francis served as a partner in the firm now known as Debevoise & Plimpton. The word "served" peculiarly fits—for intense, devoted, almost fierce service to clients, the profession and society and, indeed, to his colleagues in the firm, from the youngest on, were the touchstones of these many years.
>
> One hears of Francis as lawyer, diplomat and civic leader. We think of him also as "teacher". Seated shoulder to shoulder with a young lawyer at the drafting table, steel-rimmed glasses perched in apparent futility on the top of his head, Francis would analyze, dissect, arrange, then re-arrange—and in the end simplify—one's work. It had elements of a cold shower in that it felt better looked back on than during the process, but it was a teaching session unique and forever rewarding. Any lawyer, no matter how good, would be the better for that experience.

Much has been made of Francis' penchant for drafting—for his artistry with indentures and other complex documents. There was no arcane secret behind his prowess. It was simply a passion for excellence, accuracy, clarity and simplicity—a passion which sustained the mind and the body in the long, hard hours of work needed to achieve the quality he demanded of himself.

He struggled to achieve nuggets of brevity. Yet, he once produced a brief approaching a thousand pages. It was three or four inches thick and weighed several pounds. It was regarded by young lawyers with a mixture of fear and awe, almost as if it had taken on a life of its own. Needless to say, Francis won the case. I think the other side simply gave up.

Plimpton stories abounded, often illustrating how he turned twenty-four hours into forty-eight. Typical was the story of a young lawyer who rushed off with Francis, slightly late for an uptown meeting. Francis bounded down the subway steps, three paces ahead, as was his wont, through the doors of an arriving express. As the doors closed, the hapless associate, fumbling at the change booth, heard a cry of remonstrance surmounting the clamor—"Watkins! Always have a dime."

As the firm and the broader legal community are greatly in Francis' debt, so, obversely, it is apparent that Francis found many satisfactions with his life in the law.

The reasons, I think, can be adduced from his approaches to the law and his practice.

It was intellectually demanding because he made it so—always creative, always changing.

It gave rein to his drive for justice, and it both permitted and fostered independence. He had no master other than himself. The courage of conviction he evinced in later years, as President of the Association of the Bar of the City of New York, in initiating a Lawyers' Peace March on Washington in response to the invasion of Cambodia, reflected a lifetime of following the stars as he saw them.

Francis loved to be involved. He was our best recruiter. Even over the past two years, he participated in almost every weekly firm lunch, often gripping a rubber ball to alleviate the pain of the shingles which wracked him. In the week before he died, he expressed concern and disappointment that he and Pauline were unable to give an annual party for associates.

Finally, Francis' life in the law enmeshed him in the lives of others—their affairs, business and personal, became his concerns. Their reliance on him became his stimuli. He spent his time advising, teaching, entertaining, persuading, leading and helping people. Francis loved people.

So, in the end, it is that for which we remember him most—for the unselfish companionship, the wit and the friendship that has enriched all our lives.

George Lindsay was followed by Edward I. Koch, the Mayor of the City of New York:

I am very pleased to be here this morning as we honor the memory of Francis Plimpton, and celebrate the extraordinary life of an extraordinary New Yorker.

I had a name for Francis Plimpton. I called him "Mr. Integrity." It was the closest I could come to summing up the rare and exceptional qualities of this wonderful extraordinary person.

These qualities have served our City well over the years. Francis was appointed by Mayor Lindsay to the Board of Ethics, where he continued to serve with great distinction under Mayor Abe Beame and then under my mayoralty. It would be difficult indeed to imagine anyone more qualified to be Chairman of the Board of Ethics. One of his associates on the Board, Powell Pierpoint, called Francis "the fairest man I ever knew."

Note well the superlative in that description. Not merely "fair," or "very fair," but "the fairest man I ever knew." In a city where seven and a half million determined people are competing for advancement—and perhaps a little extra space on the Lexington Avenue local—Francis Plimpton never lost sight of the ultimate goal: to enter the arena of daily life not merely to prevail, but to prevail with decency, honor and justice.

That's why his life was a life of superlatives. He held

the high ground with courage and conviction, and others responded to his example. People didn't just "like" Francis Plimpton—they loved him. People didn't just admire him— they valued his judgment as the final word on how to get things accomplished in a way that was effective and correct. As Chairman of the Mayor's Commission for Distinguished Guests, Francis Plimpton once again brought his superlative gifts to the service of his City. New York is full of people who know lots of other people. But Francis knew everyone in the world or so it seemed. It was incredible. He also knew what to say to every one of them, and when to say it. Everything he did inspired the respect and the confidence of those around him. Last March, when I presented him with the City's La Guardia Medal, I said that, if Francis Plimpton hadn't been born a New Yorker, we would have had to consider him the most distinguished of our distinguished guests.

Today, we are honoring the memory of this remarkable man. Many people love New York City. Francis Plimpton was one of the few who was and is and will continue to be loved *by* New York City—completely, and for all time.

Then, speaking on behalf of the United Nations, Richard N. Gardner, a former Ambassador to Italy, and a friend of long standing:

Francis Plimpton served as Deputy Permanent Representative to the United Nations from January 1961 to September 1965. His first official utterance was quintessentially Francis: "I'll serve," he told the *New York Times*, "as long as my French and my digestion hold out." He called his life as U.N. diplomat "exhilarating, exhausting, exacerbating, exciting, and all the other ex's you can think of."

It was the golden age of the U.S. Mission: I doubt our country ever had a more gifted group of representatives to the world organization. First, of course, there was Adlai Stevenson, Francis' old friend and Harvard Law School classmate; then Francis, then Charles Yost, Philip Klutznick, Jonathan Bingham, Marietta Tree, Morris Abram, Jane Dick, as well as other notables.

Harold Nicolson once wrote that "the worst diplomatists

are missionairies, fanatics, and lawyers." But Harold Nicolson didn't know Francis Plimpton. Francis not only looked every inch the diplomat—tall, slender and erect, in impeccably tailored suits with a vest—he was the kind of representative we could be proud of. Adlai gave Francis the most thankless matters to handle: Arab refugees (that was before they were called Palestinians); South Africa; the U.N. financial crisis. To these and other insoluble problems, Francis brought his extraordinary professional skills as negotiator, advocate, and draftsman. Working with him was a daily lesson in clear thinking and good writing. His sound judgment of people and issues made him the perfect Deputy for Adlai.

Francis was a diplomat of the old school. He was interested, not in short-lived rhetorical victories, but in successfully fulfilling that most important of Charter purposes—"harmonizing the actions of nations." He knew how to defend the interests of the United States while showing a decent respect for the opinions and interests of others. He worked particularly hard to help us fulfill our hostship obligations in New York. It was not his style to tell foreign ambassadors that if they didn't like it here, he would stand on the dockside and wave them good-bye in the sunset.

If Adlai suffered with the U.N. social round—the "protocol, alcohol, and Geritol"—his Deputy seemed to thrive upon it. That was because Francis cared enormously about people of all varieties and was so successful in relating to them. The other delegates thought of him as a gentleman and a scholar, and most of all as a loyal and generous friend. They admired his practical wisdom and the breadth of his culture. They basked in the warm hospitality with which Francis and Pauline received them in Manhattan and Long Island. Years after he left the U.N., I had occasion to witness how his old U.N. friends would beam on meeting Francis in the Delegates' Lounge.

To be honest, Francis was not always easy for his State Department to deal with. Without any official sanction whatsoever, he went to Rome to try to convert the Pope to birth control. I once had the task of "clearing" one of his speeches on this subject to the Planned Parenthood Organization:

when the Washington bureaucracy was finished with it, every paragraph had been removed except for his opening joke. When some months later a hapless representative from the State Department—actually yours truly—was instructed to abstain in the General Assembly on the issue of granting birth control aid to developing countries, a postcard came from Singapore signed by Pauline but speaking for both of them: "Your abstention was heard 'round the world."

Surely what Dean Rusk said of Adlai Stevenson at Stevenson's memorial service applies fully to Francis:

> "It has been said that . . . he was a universal man. And so he was. But not merely because he was informed, well traveled, urbane, sophisticated, eloquent and gifted; he was all of these. But his universality did not rest upon his being a prince among plain men, but upon his being a plain man even among princes. His was the simplicity of fundamental human values—with what is permanent in the midst of change: the love of peace; the instinct of tolerance; the feeling of compassion; the devotion to human rights; the urge to act for human welfare."

But perhaps one more thing should be added. In 1971, Geoffrey Hellman, interviewing for his remarkable *New Yorker* profile, aked me for a single sentence to describe Francis. My response then was what I am thinking now: "He was the most honorable man I ever met."

G. Armour Craig, the Acting President of Amherst College, and a popular English professor, who had taught two of our sons, spoke about Francis as a trustee:

> Francis Plimpton was a trustee of trustees. He fulfilled many fiduciary roles in public life. Yet in no role perhaps was Francis more effective than in that of trustee of institutions of higher education—and in that category I include his long and devoted service to Phillips Exeter Academy as well as to Amherst, Barnard, Athens, Union Theological, and Harvard. Certainly at Amherst, in shaping the character

of which he joined with his brother in the legacy of their father, his influence will long persist, for he taught those who serve the College the very meaning of service.

His teaching was of the oldest and strongest kind: he taught by example, and he offered his example in friendship. What he expected—indeed what he exacted—of those who serve the College, was character. It may seem an old-fashioned quality to expect of your friends, but it was not—or it is not, as Francis made us understand it. Character, first of all, is something we read, as we read the characters of an alphabet or the characters of a script. Francis conceived of character first of all, I think, as what is readable in a person; it's what the younger generation terms the openness of a man or a woman. To obscure or to conceal character is to render one's text or one's self unreadable. And guile, concealment, evasion, any disguise of self-seeking behind whatever facade, Francis was ruthless and vehement in exposing. The forthright, the open, the unashamedly readable: these are some of the qualities he looked for as he sought men and women of character to instruct the young and to administer the resources that make teaching and learning possible.

Francis Plimpton not only expected character of his friends; he embodied it in his own conduct of life. In a speech to his Amherst classmates on the occasion of their fiftieth reunion he recalled for them a teacher they had known and admired in the early twenties: "One felt an inner lift," he said, "from the uncompromising, undeviating directness of his insistence on the search for the truth no matter where that search might lead." And in so saying Francis was bearing witness to a kind of strength that he intimately recognized, for he had it himself. The figure for Francis must be a little different, though the strength is the same, for his strength issued not in an undeviating directness of insistence but rather in a constant shining forth that was unshadowed. Not all men who have occupied such positions or exercised such power as Francis did are so serene, so secure, so strong as to refuse to traffic with the gestures of connivance and concealment with which we are so frequently surrounded. To guide the young, to educate those who will constitute our future, he wanted men and women who are not afraid to be read, who in the fullest sense have nothing to hide. Francis Plimpton's own character, the public contours of self for all to read, was graceful and strong. He was a splendid, shining man whose example altered the conduct of the many lives whom he touched with his trust. All of us who knew him will in our turn feel an inner lift as we remember the constancy of his shining forth.

Then, our son, George Plimpton finished the program by speaking on behalf of the family:

There are those who must wonder—considering how much time father gave to the public family of man—how he could ever have managed a private family of his own. But he did, as you know. He was never able to turn any of his four children to an abiding interest in the law—perhaps, I have always thought, because he tended to give his lecture on the beauty of the mortgage indenture, and indeed its position as the very cornerstone of the legal culture, at breakfast.

So he gave up on that. But he in everything else encouraged us. He cajoled us to be better, to be disciplined. He taught us the Continental backhand, perhaps the last youths in the East to learn such a thing. He wrote us wonderful letters when we went away to school—about the machinery of the mind, and what delight there was in the results of its functioning at its best.

And best of all, he made us see the pleasure of the challenge.

He loved challenges of all kinds—especially those which engaged the mind. You have heard many instances in the tributes which have preceded. I remember when he received the Légion d'Honneur—a tribute he was tremendously proud of and wore the red ribbon on his seersucker coat, as many of you know, at summer lunches at West Hills. He chose to give his acceptance speech at the French Consulate in French, in which he was a little bit rusty. What made it a particular challenge was that in his speech he told a funny story. That is truly a challenge—to tell a funny story in

rusty French to a room full of French dignitaries. I will tell
you the story, but not in French. I did not learn that much
courage from my father. It was a story about the difficulty
of communication—a United Nations kind of story. Father
described how he had gone to a movie theatre off the Champs
Elysées where an American Western was being shown in
English with the subtitles in French. At one point a gun-
slinger, a very rough sort, had shot up a bar, his guns
blazing, and afterwards had swaggered up to the bar where
he said, "Gimme a shot of red-eye!" The subtitle to translate
this read as follows: "Donnez-moi un Dubonnet, s'il vous
plaît."

Coupled with this love of challenge was a tremendous
sense of tradition . . . that there were certain verities worth
cultivating and preserving. In his 70's, I suggested that he
shift tennis racquets—giving up his small-headed model
which he had used for decades, always returning it properly
to its wooden press, for one of the big Prince racquets that
were coming into vogue then. In fact, I gave him one for
Christmas. He was very polite about receiving it, but he
never used it. Possibly he thought that it would give him
an unfair advantage, but I think more probably it meant
giving up an old and faithful ally that along with mother's
forehand had carried him to a steady succession of cham-
pionships at the Cold Spring Harbor Beach Club. So he
kept to his old racquet—which was called a Power Bat.
Rarely has the English language, he once told me, with the
possible exception of that of the mortgage indenture, been
used so succinctly to describe what he wished of it. I remember telling him once that Althea Gibson used a Power
Bat. He nodded and said, "A woman of exceptional
judgment."

I remember father once saying to me that life was especially worth living for the surprises that come along from
time to time. I know of my own generation, and those
succeeding that in their letters of condolence so many have
mentioned meeting father for the first time—and of the
pleasure and surprise of running into such an inquiring,
attentive, humorous and courtly mind, and coming away
with the warm and abiding pleasure of being so much the

better for the experience of having met him. And the breadth
of his capacities! So many of the wives, not only of his
own generation, have so often remarked on what a dancer
my father was—now *there* was an experience!

My son Taylor, who was six at the time, brought a large
handkerchief to Walpole, tucked enormously in the breast
pocket of his school blazer, to the funeral services there
because he thought it was appropriate to weep on such
occasions. But here, today, of course, we find ourselves at
a kind of celebration—to sit here in the pews of this church
and to recall how fortunate all of us here have been—family,
friends, dancing partners, statesmen, civic leaders, club-
mates, politicians, educators, students, lawyers, justices,
citizens—to have been touched by the presence of this remarkable person, husband and parent.

One is reminded of what Callimachus said of the death
of Heraclitus: "Oh, Heraclitus, they tell me you are dead,
but I know you are not gone. Thy nightingales live on. I
hear them sing . . .''

Index

UNESCO, 43
UNICEF, 43
Uniform State Laws
 Committee, Association
 of the Bar of the City
 of New York, 76
Union Club, 82
Union Internationale des
 Avocats (U.I.A.), 118
Union Theological
 Seminary, 117, 118,
 130
United Nations, 32–33, 97–
 98, 113, 128
United Nations Conciliation
 Commission for
 Palestine, 36, 37
United States Mission to the
 United Nations
 (USUN), 59, 60–61
United States Trust
 Company, 117
UNRWA, 43
Ustor, Endre, 67, 67
U Thant, 38, 43, 44, 45–46,
 49, 52–54, 62, 66

Van Fleet, General, 63
Veblen, Thorstein, 12
Venkataraman, R., 67
Vermont Law School, 12, 14

Wabash Railroad, 5
Waldheim, Kurt, 55
Waldorf Astoria Towers,
 New York City, 31, 59,
 121

Walker, Edwin, 113
Ward, William, 118
Warren, Charles, 72
Warren, Earl, 72–74
Washington Post, 88
Waterman, Sterry, 13
Webster, Bethuel M., xxvi,
 80, 82, 83
Webster, Sheffield,
 Fleischmann, Hitchcock
 & Brookfield, 80
Wellesley Club of New
 York, xvii
Wellesley College, xvii,
 xviii
West Irian crisis, 43
Willkie, Wendell, 72
Woodin, W. H., 6
Woolcott, Alexander, xxvi
World Bank, 43, 104
World Court, 93
World Meteorological
 Organization, 43
World Peace Through Law,
 93

Yale Law School, xxiii, 80,
 83
Yemen crisis, 52
Yost, Charles, 66, 66, 128
Young, Stark, xxiii

Zorin, V., 38, 47, 51, 64,
 65